Going Public

Going Public

An Organizer's Guide to Citizen Action

MICHAEL GECAN

ANCHOR BOOKS

A DIVISION OF RANDOM HOUSE, INC.

NEW YORK

FIRST ANCHOR BOOKS EDITION, MAY 2004

Copyright © 2002 by Michael Gecan

All rights reserved under International and Pan-American Copyright
Conventions. Published in the United States by Anchor Books, a division
of Random House, Inc., New York, and simultaneously in Canada by
Random House of Canada Limited, Toronto. Originally published in
hardcover in the United States by Beacon Press, Boston, in 2002.

Library of Congress Cataloging-in-Publication Data
Gecan, Michael.
Going public / Michael Gecan
p. cm.
Originally published: Boston : Beacon Press, c2002
Includes bibliographical references and index.
ISBN 1-4000-7649-8
1. Community development—United States—Case studies.
2. Community organization—United States—Case studies.
3. Industrial Areas Foundation. I. Title.
HN90.C6G43 2004
307.1'4'0973—dc22
2003063568

Author photograph © Nora Gecan

www.anchorbooks.com

Printed in the United States of America
10 9 8 7 6 5 4 3 2

Going Public

"Trained by Saul Alinsky, whose *Rules for Radicals* is the original handbook for grassroots organizing, Gecan . . . show[s] the incredible power people can have over their own lives and their own government when they stand together in creative ways. He exposes, through anecdotes, the themes of the book: the importance of building meaningful public relationships through individual, formal meetings; the necessity of understanding, and accepting as the rules of the game, the realpolitik of government, no matter how just your own cause is." —*America*

"A compact, instructional guide that effectively updates Saul Alinsky's *Reveille for Radicals* and *Rules for Radicals* for the twenty-first century." —*Library Journal*

"The inside story of an extraordinary politics you probably didn't know existed. Read this book and you may begin to believe that human-scale democracy is still possible in America." —William Greider, author of *Who Will Tell the People: The Betrayal of American Democracy*

"This is a classic! *Going Public* is an engaging, informative, and entertaining book with a message for all who are called on to organize to make a difference, whether in their community or their company. These insights from a consummate organizer are both a 'how to' and a 'why to' primer for anyone who wants to have an impact."
—Tom Wheeler, author of *Take Command! Leadership Lessons from the Civil War*

MICHAEL GECAN

Going Public

Michael Gecan has worked as an organizer for the
Industrial Areas Foundation (IAF) in New York,
Chicago, Philadelphia, and Baltimore for more
than twenty-five years. Gecan lives in Princeton,
New Jersey.

FOR SHEILA

CONTENTS

PART IV: The Habit of Reflection

Going Public

I am an organizer. It's a strange word—"organizer"—a word from the past, a black-and-white photo of a person passing out fliers to workers leaving an auto plant.

But it's 2002, and I am an organizer. Not a consultant to so-called faith-based programs. Not a facilitator. Not an adviser. Not a service provider or do-gooder. Not an ideologue. Not a political operative. Not a pundit. Not a progressive. Not an activist.

I'm clearly not a lot of things. In my organizing, I use other old-fashioned words like "leader" and "follower," "power" and "action," "confrontation" and "negotiation," "relationships" and "institutions." These words still form the phonics of the larger language of politics.

With these basic tools, the plots and subplots of public life, no matter how intricate, begin to make sense. Characters come to life. Motivations emerge. Relationships reveal themselves. Themes and story lines become clear. The reader can begin to talk back to the teller of the tale, can begin to judge, or can pick up a pen and create a different world. In the public arena, participation and action and change can take place.

But *I* won't begin to make sense unless I follow the advice of my former college professor and poet laureate, the late Robert Penn Warren, and tell some stories. We took a walk one day on the Connecticut roads near his Fairfield home. It was a brisk winter afternoon, and his dog was yanking him along. As we walked, he provided a gentle but thorough critique of a novel I was working on at the time. He kept coming back to a simple theme: "Just tell the story. Forget everything else and tell your story." He was repeating what he had already written in his wonderful book-length poem, *Audubon: A Vision*, "Tell me a story. / In this century, and moment, of mania, / Tell me a story / . . . Tell me a story of deep delight." So, many years later, I will follow the advice of this wise teacher and tell you some stories from my life, the beginnings of my life as an organizer.

I grew up on the west side of Chicago in the fifties and learned that we live in a world of power—raw power—long before I knew the word. My mother and father bought a tavern when my sister and I were quite young. As a six-year-old, I served shots and beers to the men who sat along "my" section of the bar. My customers were Italians, Irish, and fellow Croatians. They walked down the hill a block away from the Chicago and Northwestern Railroad yard at noon—for a couple of shots, a couple of beers, and sandwiches and soup made by my mother in the kitchen. My father built a small platform behind the bar so that I could serve my crowd.

I remember this as a glorious time in my life—a time when I was admitted to an adult world of strength and laughter and toughness. (My parents remember this as a period of unremitting pressure and endless work.) The time ended on a sunny afternoon. The young man from the mob came in to pick up his monthly payment. My father explained to him that, because by mother had taken ill, we were short. As my father and the young man talked, all the other men at the bar became silent, looked down at their drinks, or stared straight ahead. The young man told my father that he knew what he had to do. My father nodded. Then the man turned around and walked out. Slowly, conversation picked back up. Someone ordered a shot of vo and a Schlitz. That night, my father closed the bar—Gus's Tavern—for good.

No matter where you turned, you ran smack into people with power. The power of the mob. The power of the police. The power of the Cook County Democratic Party—which demanded three hundred dollars from every working man in our neighborhood who sought a city job. Three hundred dollars was a lot of money in those days. And all that it bought was a place "on the list." No one knew for sure, but the sense was that a small percentage of people eventually got jobs. The rest paid off, sat silently, and had nowhere to go and no one to complain to when their payoff didn't work.

Life on the street was no different. As a white, working-class boy, I grew up fighting black, working-class boys. We jumped them. They jumped us. We feared them. And we wanted them to fear us. Our lives were strictly circumscribed—divided by el lines, railroad tracks, and major thoroughfares. Cross any border and you had to be prepared to pay the price. Every aspect of our upbringing taught us either to avoid or to confront one another.

Our lives were a series of serious and sudden skirmishes. One afternoon, two friends and I were sitting on a curb. In the distance, three blacks, about our age, walked along Ferdinand Street, toward us. They ambled, it seemed to me then and in memory, incredibly slowly and casually. As they approached, the toughest of our three, Mike Stepkovicz, now dead, pulled out his knife, opened it behind his back, and waited. No one moved until they were right in front of us. Then Stecks, short and stocky but quick as a snake, grabbed the lead boy, put the knife to his neck, and asked him where the fuck he thought he was going. The boy's eyes were wide, unblinking. No words came out of his mouth, although his lips moved. The rest of us just froze. As quickly as he struck, Stecks let the kid go and told him to head back the same way he came. We watched them walk away, faster now, back toward Pulaski Road, south toward Lake Street, out of our turf, out of our sight.

And there was the much more complicated power of large institutions—particularly the Roman Catholic Church. Our parish, Our Lady of the Angels, anchored our lives. It's where we prayed, socialized, played bingo, went to school. This same parish—and scores like it—often turned a blind eye to the needs of the working-class whites who packed its schools and sanctuaries.

I watched as my mother tried to convince our local pastor to do something about the real estate hustlers who were panicking white families to leave the neighborhood by warning of the impending flood of black buyers. These hustlers spoke every language we spoke—Croatian, Italian, German, and Czechoslovakian. They called every day, many times a day, and then into the evening, and then all through the night. They roused bone-tired factory workers from their beds to alert them to how much their home had lost in value that week, to make them one last offer. Exhaustion and fear grew. Neighbors moved suddenly, without a word of warning. Then panic spread. The real estate agents bought low from our families and sold high to black families eager for a better and safer life for their children. They ravaged entire sections of a once great city—several times over. They drove families like mine from neighborhood to neighborhood, two, three, and four times, further west and northwest and southwest toward the suburbs, losing more equity, hope, and faith each time. Then they bankrupted black and Hispanic buyers and steered them into new ghettoes.

My mother went to the pastor and described all this. He nodded and said he would get back to her. He never did. We found out later that he essentially redrew the lines of the parish to exclude our four square blocks, which turned from nearly entirely white to nearly entirely black in one traumatic and violent summer in the late sixties. We didn't move for three more years because my Croatian grandmother, who owned our house, and who would have survived the bombing of Vukovar, refused to leave.

My mother's actions introduced me to a different kind of power—an attempt by someone to defend herself and her family, to enlist other families in the effort, to research an issue and understand it well, to take that research and analysis to a place where she thought her work would be welcome. She did all this with a positive spirit. She related as openly to our new black neighbors as to our fleeing white friends. Deeply disappointed by the inaction of the pastor, she didn't use that disappointment as a reason to retreat from all public matters or to reject her local parish or her larger church.

It would have been understandable if she had rejected them. She had already survived one tragedy. On the first day of December in 1958, the parish school, packed with sixteen hundred kids, caught fire. Ninety-five people died that day—ninety-two children and three nuns.

I recall the sights and sounds of that first of December nearly every day of my life. A siren, a news story, a charred building in Brooklyn, schoolchildren waiting on line or racing around an asphalt playground, inanities from the mouth of a public official trying to avoid responsibility—it doesn't take much to jog my memory.

Once again, I am one of fifty or so fourth graders sitting in a crowded classroom copying the perfect script of Sr. Mary Edgar . . . "Geography. Read page fifty-eight . . ." She is tall and thin and strictly upright, just like the tall and elegant letters on the board. Then, the fire alarm rings, late in the afternoon, just before dismissal, which makes us all groan and grumble quietly. We will have to walk outside without our coats and wait until the entire school empties and then go back in and dress for the end of the day. In other words, we will leave later than usual.

But today there will be no going back for coats and books and backpacks. As we file into the hallway, we look up the wide stairwell leading to the second floor. Midway down, smoke, thick as muscle, blocks our view. The groaning and grumbling stop. We hurry out to the sidewalk in front of the school and follow our leader along Iowa Street toward the church. As we walk, we glance back, see smoke pouring from windows.

In the church, we are commanded to kneel and pray—600, 800, 1,000, 1,200, and more frightened kids, more packed in every minute. We can hear windows breaking, muffled screams, and thuds from the school fifty yards away. Someone in my group of friends says, "Let's get out of here, see if we can help." So we slip out of the pew. We rush, crouching, down the aisle—a small pack of ten-year-old boys sneaking through the crush of arriving children.

A moment later, we find that we have hurried into a holocaust. Sirens wail from every direction, as if the whole city is keening. The next hour is a blur. We are wandering among the bodies beginning to crowd the sidewalk in front of the school. We are sent into a nearby house. Later, we are running, coatless, bookless, home, running six blocks against a rising tide of parents and brothers and sisters and neighbors, who are pouring toward the school.

The crush of fire trucks and ambulance snarled traffic right into the rush hour. My father, like hundreds of other parents, heard this terrible news about the school but could not get home because of the tie-ups. Finally, when he rushed into the house, hours late, covered with lime dust from his day as a plasterer, he looked like a ghost, as did my younger sister and I. He had seen so much death and near-death, from Omaha Beach to the Battle of the Bulge, but nothing had left him feeling so desolate and helpless, he said, as the endless hours of that afternoon.

Out on the street, in front of the school, a young priest named Jack Egan performed last rites and comforted the barely living and consoled the parents who were already beyond consolation, and would remain that way, some of them, haunted for the rest of their lives.

When ninety-two children die in one neighborhood, along with three religious women who taught them, the entire community mourns. In this case, the "community" extended beyond the streets and avenues of the west side, beyond Springfield and Avers and Harding and Thomas, beyond Augusta and Iowa and Erie, beyond the modest row houses and crowded bungalows and gray two-flats, beyond the decade and the century in which it occurred. In this case, the community included the rest of the city, Catholic schools everywhere, and people of all cities and states. The children of the city were dead—the kind of kids who lived in every American city at the time. Their photos filled the entire front page of one of the city's newspapers a few days later. The event had the impact of the Triangle Shirtwaist Fire—another instance of tragic loss among working-class women in a New York City knitting mill. Fire safety rose to the top of the national agenda. Dioceses and schools districts campaigned for sprinkler systems and other fire safety solutions.

But there was a terrible twist to this tragedy. The OLA fire wasn't caused by an abusive employer showing disregard for his workers. In the city of Chicago, in 1958, Roman Catholic schoolchildren, in their local parish school, in a Roman Catholic city, led by a mayor who attended Mass each and every morning, died unnecessarily. The institution that sometimes gave life, through adoption services; saved life, through their health care and hospitals; supported and enriched life, through their schools and seminaries—this same institution exposed its most faithful followers to firetrap conditions and the possibility of injury and death.

When the west side of Chicago—and scores of neighborhoods like it in many American cities—began to burn again, in the mid-sixties, just ten years after the OLA fire, when parish after parish experienced a near-total turnover in a matter of months, when hundreds of thousands of hardworking ethnic Catholics were driven from their homes and hundreds of thousands of hardworking blacks and Hispanics were steered in, I saw the same kind of deadly disregard—only this time a little less dramatic, less stunning to the senses. This time, it was politicians benefiting from the profiteering of real estate hustlers. This time it was arsonists working for panic peddlers and landlords. This time, it was stunned and frightened pastors and rabbis drawing and redrawing the lines of their shrinking congregations until they had no people left to serve. This time, tragedy didn't strike in an hour on a December afternoon; the burning went on for a decade—a long, slow smolder that caused far more damage than the spasms of violence experienced in the late sixties—and left hundreds of neighborhoods and scores of cities trashed.

For every example of an abuse of power, I experienced, often by accident, an alternative way to wield power. A few years after the fight with the three black kids on Ferdinand Street, I found myself stepping tentatively into a black Baptist church—taken there by a Jesuit Scholastic who taught at my mostly white Roman Catholic high school. We were neither avoided nor confronted there. We were welcomed, acknowledged, accepted, and encouraged. We were then treated to a wonderful worship service—the first of many in my life as an organizer. Here, too, was power—organization and talent, leadership and discipline, external impact and real change. And here was music and humor and warmth that I had not yet felt in any other church.

Not long after my mother's encounter with our local pastor, I read about Fr. Jack Egan in the Sunday paper. It was now the late sixties and Egan was serving as the pastor of Presentation Parish, just two miles south of our home. He was also one of the guiding spirits behind a growing black homeowners group called the Contract Buyers League. With leaders like Ruth Wells and Clyde Ross, another young Jesuit named Jack Macnamara, and a staff of college-age summer interns, Egan and company were working to correct the conditions that occurred when homes were sold on contract at exorbitant prices to minority buyers. A contract sale meant that the buyer had no equity *until he or she made the last payment.* At any time before that, the buyer could lose everything if a payment was missed or even late. This process thrived because the federal government allowed lending institutions to withhold conventional financing—a process called redlining—from working-class communities all across the country. It was sanctioned by the great Cook County Democratic Party, which sacrificed the financial stability and peace of mind of hundreds of thousands of its most loyal followers for the payoffs, prostitutes, and cases of bourbon provided by the mortgage bankers, title attorneys, real estate sharks, and savings and loan executives.

Face to face with this formidable array of opponents, in an archdiocese that brooked no action or dissent at the time, stood Jack Egan and Jack Macnamara and the indomitable leaders of Lawndale. They organized hundreds of homeowners every Wednesday night in the basement of the parish church. They picketed savings and loans in Cicero while heavily armed federal marshals separated them from rabid white crowds. They challenged the major Chicago banks that held the contracts for these speculators to reveal the extent of the abuse. And they eventually forced those who profited from this urban erosion to repay hundreds of home-owners' families.

So, before I went off to college, I saw power in several forms. I saw the mafia punk in the bar—just another soldier in an army of power abusers who burdened our family and humiliated our father and tried to break our spirit. And I saw my mother preparing for her meeting with our pastor, black homeowners like Ruth Wells picking up the pieces in Lawndale, and a young minister in a Baptist church preaching a sermon on civil rights in a city both hostile to his message and elaborately organized to frustrate him.

I sensed that you couldn't just "reform" the abusers of power, legislate against them, sue them into submission, or sway them with the merits of your case. I sensed that you had to battle them —power against power, institution against institution—to check them and counter them and ensure that your vision of society and community, rooted in the best blend of democratic and religious traditions, had a chance to grow and survive from season to season and year to year.

And I began to see—although this notion emerged more gradually over many years—that organizing, participating, and acting were essential to the health of your own institutions, your own congregation or faith, your own political party or union, your own association or citizens organization, not just the institutions run by those you believe to be neutral or hostile to your interests. All institutions tend to drift. There's always the danger of the easy wink between the pastor and the fire inspector, between the lobbyist and the senator, between the corporate contributor and the chief of staff, between the not-for-profit executive and agency head. No technical reform or legal sanction or government regulation can stop this. No degree of separation and individual avoidance can insulate a person from the consequences of these insider trades and institutional shifts.

So leaders and organizers face a tough challenge: maintaining a conservative's belief in the value and necessity of stable institutions, along with a radical's understanding of the need for persistent agitation and reorganization. We are called to love, engage, and uphold our most cherished institutions, while watching them, questioning them, and pressing them to change, all at the same time.

The women and men who resist the temptation to choose one extreme or the other, or who don't just opt out, are every bit as important to the defense of this democracy, in times of crisis and times of peace, as the dogged citizen soldiers who landed on Omaha Beach. Many are already in the field and gaining ground. Millions more are willing to fight, even itching to, but feel as if they lack the training or the language or the skills to do so effectively. And many of these new American leaders, these soldierly citizens, just don't know where to sign up or how to start. This book is about how to do just that.

About fifteen years ago, the Senate was considering a series of issues relating to immigration. Leaders and organizers from our groups in Texas, New York, and California were concerned. Four leaders from New York—two Roman Catholic priests and two Hispanic lay leaders—and I took the early shuttle to Washington and arrived about fifteen minutes before the hearing was scheduled to begin. We wandered through hallways—tunnels without subways, one of our leaders said—until we spotted a long line of people along one wall. More than 150 men and women moved toward the large double doors of the hearing room.

Guarding the door was a tall, affable security officer who leaned over every so often to those preparing to enter. He said something to each individual or group, nodded his head at the answer, and then waved them in. When we got to the guard, he leaned toward us and asked, "Lobbyists or staff?"

We were all silent for a moment. Then, I said, "Citizens."

"Ha!" he roared, to all those who had formed behind us and to the world at large, "Get this: we got some citizens here!" The hallway echoed with knowing laughter.

The second story took place around the same time, in New York City. A Lutheran pastor and eight members of his congregation were planning to go to City Hall to attend a session of what was then the most important governing body there—the now-defunct Board of Estimate. The congregation hoped to acquire a nearby abandoned building and renovate it for church programs. It learned that the city was about to dispose of the structure to another group and that this disposition would be an agenda item during the day's meeting.

I asked the pastor if I could tag along. I was new to the city at the time, had never been to the Board of Estimate, and wanted to get a sense of how things worked there. When I arrived at City Hall the next day, I was impressed by the elegance of the Board of Estimate chamber. It had high ceilings, eight chairs stationed behind a raised dais, fixed wooden pews for the citizens waiting for the proceedings to begin, and a thick altar rail separating those attending from those presiding. On the far left end of the altar rail was a small Dutch door, with a sign saying "DO NOT ENTER," in stark stern letters.

The pastor and his people were all carrying bag or box lunches with them, along with books, newspapers, magazines, and knitting materials. Everything about them—their supplies, their comfortable clothes, their soft shoes—communicated that they were expecting a long day. When I inquired, they clued me in. The meetings often ran from ten in the morning, which time it was, until two or three the next morning; that there were 520 items in an agenda that looked like the course catalog for a major university; and that you never really knew when your item would be dealt with—on first call, which meant while the sun still shone, or during the dreaded second call, when meant in the wee hours.

I groaned silently, glanced toward the dais again, and noticed that every five seconds or so someone was pushing through the door with the DO NOT ENTER sign on it. I asked the pastor who those people were. He said, "Must be staff." But I had never seen staff so well dressed, confident, and prosperous looking. They would march through the door as if it weren't there, mount the dais behind the eight chairs, and kibitz with one another, with the board members, and with other younger people who did look like staff to me.

I asked the pastor, "Why don't we go up there and find out what's going to happen to your building?"

"We can't," he said. "The sign says DO NOT ENTER."

Before you get the wrong idea about this pastor, let me tell you right here that this is one of the toughest and bravest men that I have ever had the pleasure of meeting. He rode a bicycle around the mean streets of East Brooklyn, at all hours, to visit the sick and lonely and troubled, who often seemed to find their way to him. He was a stocky Texan with a long German name who wore a beret and carried a Bible and was undaunted by the broken elevators in Howard Houses when he received an emergency call at three in the morning. But this tough Texan would not go through the little Dutch door that day.

So I went. Pushed the door. Strode past the guard. Climbed the short stairs. Sidestepped through the crush of people to position myself just to the side of the Brooklyn borough president's representative. I asked his chief of staff about the item that brought the Lutheran leaders there that day. He leaned back, without looking at me, and growled, "We're tabling it. Go home. We'll deal with it at next month's meeting." I relayed the message to the pastor and his people, who were thrilled to learn of their reprieve. They packed up and returned to their jobs, families, parish duties, and community. The clock read a quarter past ten.

This is my business. I encourage, coach, and agitate citizens to play their rightful roles and claim their rightful places in the public

arena of our nation. It's an arena that sends mixed and contradic-
tory messages to people. Although it boasts the promise and symbols, the bureaucratic structures and legislative processes, of full
and open participation, it is positively packed with paid lobbyists
and paid staff. Its doors and rooms are plastered with signs that
warn DO NOT ENTER. It is a place where people are routinely told to
be patient, told to wait, told to come back next month, where people are crowded out, discouraged from voting, and are frustrated in
their attempts to be complete and responsible citizens. It provides
pews for the people to sit in and watch but erects multiple barriers
to meaningful engagement.

There's a powerful and fundamental tension between our political rhetoric and rituals and our everyday actions and practices
—a tension written into our founding documents and present in
most of our public crises. The organizer lives with and within that
tension, challenges citizens to confront it, and schemes with them
to honor the best of our political traditions by pushing the political
world as it is in the direction of the world as it ought to be.

I am one of about 150 full-time professional organizers working with the Industrial Areas Foundation, founded by the late Saul
D. Alinsky in 1940. We have helped build and staff more than sixty
citizens' organizations in twenty states and the District of Colum-
bia. Our groups are made up of nearly three thousand congregations and associations and tens of thousands of ministers, pastors,
rabbis, women religious, and top lay and civic leaders. Several million Americans, from Brownsville, Texas, to Brownsville, Brooklyn, call themselves members of our groups. These members are
African American and Hispanic, white and Asian. They are individuals on the edge of homelessness, as well as families in upper-
middle-class communities in Montgomery County, Maryland, or
north suburban Chicago. They are Democrats, Republicans, and

Independents, more often than not in the moderate middle of the political spectrum.

They do not have an opportunity to do what citizens did in 1860, in a period when public debate was of the highest quality and public engagement at its most intense. They don't walk or ride great distances with their neighbors, stand by the thousands in the hot sun, hear Douglass and Lincoln debate, then argue among themselves about the issues of the day. But they do the next best thing: they spend untold hours mastering and using the full range of public arts and skills. They learn how to listen to others, to teach and train their members and followers, to think and reflect on the issues and pressures of the day, to confront those in power who obstruct or abuse them, and to build lasting relationships with allies who support or reinforce them. As leaders in large and effective citizens organizations, they practice how to argue, act, negotiate, and compromise.

These are normal and commonsensical people, people who have rich and full lives in their families and congregations and in their workplaces and communities. They are not activists, for the most part. They are not ideologues. They appreciate the market, often work in the private sector, and value the important place that the market occupies in any vital society. But they don't worship it, don't put profit above all else, and don't believe greed is good.

These citizens don't genuflect before another modern idol— the bureaucratic state. They don't dream of a society of large programs and pompous administrators. They don't believe that bigger government is necessarily better. They don't value paper and procedure and patronage. In fact, they and their families suffer most when cities, counties, and federal agencies are run and staffed by political hacks.

Nor do they see themselves as another faction, party, or sect—

Nader raiders or Perot followers. They don't pledge allegiance to a single issue or single leader. They don't believe a secular messiah, no matter how gifted or talented, can fix all that ails them. They are not just trying to elect one of their own and squeeze her or him into the small room behind the door that says DO NOT ENTER.

In fact, these people, often overlooked, are themselves "leaders" in almost every sense of the word. They have the trust and loyalty of others who follow them. They have passion and persistence. They know how to put a situation in perspective and laugh at it and themselves. They care about their local communities and interests but also search for ways to contribute to their cities, counties, and nation.

And they operate in an area of society that many Americans either doubt the existence of or can't name. Management guru Peter Drucker called it simply "the third sector." It's the large and growing sector of voluntary organizations—of congregations, associations, sports leagues, and service groups. It's a sector that figures out how to do what the market or state have either shown no interest in doing or have failed to do well. It's a sector whose product—the growth and development of people and their voluntary institutions—is often not recognized, often underappreciated, occasionally patted on the head and offered token "offices of faith-based solutions," and at other times actively undermined.

It's a sector that succeeds, when it does, not just because it is "faith-based." Some groups are and some are not. And many so-called "faith-based" organizations perform quite poorly. It's a sector that succeeds, when it does, not just because it is smaller and more local. While the best third sector groups are local, many are not small at all. It's a sector that succeeds because its leaders have learned how to manufacture and manage power—the ability to act—consistently and effectively. Not the power to abuse others back. Not the power to dominate. Not the power to replace the last bully with a new bully. Not the power to keep others from entering. But the power to demand recognition and reciprocity and respect, the power to create and sustain meaningful public relationships.

Unlike almost everyone else in the public arena, except perhaps utility executives, they don't shy away from using the problematic word "power." Here's a recent example. The assistant to a university president called. We had scheduled a meeting with the president, and the assistant was preparing a briefing sheet for him. She had already done some research on us, so she began by saying that she understood that our group was a kind of community development organization. I said that it was no such thing. It was a power organization.

"A what?" she asked, as if she hadn't heard me clearly.

"A power organization—a citizens power organization."

"What's that?"

"What's what?"

"Power."

"It's the ability to act—on a whole range of issues, in a variety of ways. . . ."

It would have been easier to let her description—innocently offered and partly true—stand. Just as it would be easier to explain to any curious person or inquiring reader that we are a housing organization, an education reform coalition, or a faith-based group. We would then fit more neatly into the current map of the world. But the predictable world pictured there is flat and incomplete. It lacks curves and contours and entire continents of political reality still undiscovered and unexplored.

This became clear to me many years ago, when an associate invited me to a gathering of housing organizations in Brooklyn. When we arrived, we had a difficult time finding seats in an auditorium packed with three hundred executives and staff members from local development groups. I was stunned and a little perplexed; I had no idea that there were so many people managing so many groups. The vast majority seemed decent, earnest, honestly interested in tackling the enormous challenge of rebuilding devastated communities. They had briefcases and development plans and phone and fax numbers neatly printed on business cards. They went to offices and answered calls. They chaired meetings and attended conferences. They raised money from foundations and won contracts from government agencies. They even identified buildings or sites that they sought to control or develop. But the reason I was surprised by the size of the crowd was that, at the time, no one was building or renovating housing on any scale whatsoever. Sadly, the people in the room had everything but the essential thing—the power to produce.

When you say that you seek power, want power, you are heading into terra incognita. You are no longer a do-gooder holding hands with your brothers and sisters and singing "Kumbaya." You aren't an earnest private in Colin Powell's volunteer army looking for a fence to paint or a chance to help those in need. You're not satisfied with just having access to power, thrilled by the visitation of a politician to your congregation. You see no reason to operate through intermediaries and flaks handpicked by the insiders and sanctioned by the media.

When you say that you have power and intend to use it, you signal your dissatisfaction with the way the two other major sectors in society—the private sector and the public sector—are handling certain matters. And you present an implicit challenge: you are ready and willing to show the other sectors how to tackle those matters more effectively.

Of course, then you stop being a spectator, a critic, or a high-minded activist with a rational analysis, supporting data, and six enlightened recommendations. You get off the couch and out of the stands. You enter the arena and place yourself squarely in the mix—as a fellow owner of what may or may not happen, as some-one willing to be *held* accountable, not just hold others account-able. You become more engaged, more suspect, more threatening, and more exposed.

But it's all just talk—this use of the word "power," just like so many other rhetorical claims—unless it is reinforced by the habit and practice of organizing. That's why, when we are called by the neighborhood or religious leaders of a city, we tell them that we won't come to solve a housing problem or an education problem or a low-wage problem. No, we say we'll try to help them solve a more fundamental problem—a power problem. No matter how terrible the conditions may be and no matter how intense the current crisis, we will spend a year or two or three with them *not* addressing these immediate and important issues and concerns. We'll use that time to build the organization and to develop a firm base of power, so that the group will someday have the punch and impact needed to instigate and preserve lasting change.

That's what Ed Chambers, the occasionally gruff and blustery director of the Industrial Areas Foundation (IAF), who was Alin-sky's protégé, told a group of tough and impatient leaders in 1978, when they called from East Brooklyn and said that they wanted to organize. Alinsky was extraordinarily effective as a tactician, writer, speaker, and gadfly. He was the first theorist and exponent of citizens organizing in urban communities. In fact, he was so effective at stirring people and provoking reaction that I still get angry calls from disgruntled people wondering where they can find that SOB Alinsky. They seem disappointed when I point out that Alinsky died, in California, in 1972. While Alinsky had many gifts and strengths—among them the ability to make indelible impressions—he did not create organizations that endured.

That was Chambers's critical contribution to the world of citi-zens organizing and to America as a whole. He had a talent for teaching people how to organize power that lasted. He had faith in their ability to build a machine that had a soul. So, when the call came from East Brooklyn, Chambers agreed to fly there from his headquarters in Chicago and meet with a team of embattled ministers and community leaders.

In the spring of 1978, East Brooklyn was the South Bronx minus the presidential motorcades. It was a place of stunning devastation, glaring needs. Gunfire crackled every night. There was fire, abandonment, and rubble. In the words of one visitor, Boston's Mayor White, it looked like "the beginning of the end of civilization." The leaders that met with Ed Chambers that day were eager, even desperate, to do something, anything, now.

Chambers heard the leaders out. Then he told them precisely what they did not want to hear. Forget the issues. Don't pick a galvanizing cause. Avoid charismatic leadership. Instead, he urged them to take the time to recruit more local congregations and associations in the area, so that they would begin to reflect the racial and religious diversity in a community of nearly a quarter of a million people. He preached financial independence that began with each and every member institution, no matter how poor and pressed, shelling out significant yearly dues to the fledgling organization. Only after the local leaders and institutions committed their money—dues money, hard money—should they pursue softer foundation funding. He set a high target: $250,000 in money raised and money pledged. And he insisted that they never seek government funding for their core budget. Finally, he challenged them to take the time to learn about power and how it really works and to focus more on the growth and development of local leaders.

Chambers hammered away: recruit institutions; find allies; pay dues; train leaders; don't do for others what they can do for themselves. Some in the group grumbled. How could they ask their followers to pay dues to an organization that wasn't ready to address issues? Chamber answered their question with another question: how could *they* ask people for tithes and offerings to support their local congregations? Because they believed in what they were preaching and teaching. Because people, no matter how poor, always found ways to pay for what they truly valued. And when they paid for it with their own hard-earned money, not the government's, not some foundation's, they owned it. And ownership—of a home, a congregation, an organization, a nation—encouraged participation and responsibility, accountability and commitment.

The activists squirmed, fumed, and rebelled. Without an issue or cause or crisis, no one would act, no one would move, and no one would work. You have to "prove" to people that success is possible before asking them to join, pay dues, or attend training. Chambers conceded that that was the conventional wisdom in the progressive and radical worlds. But in this case the conventional wisdom was dead wrong. Loose groupings of interested individuals didn't have a prayer of addressing major crises—housing, crime, schools, jobs, and others. Each crisis was, at bottom, a power crisis. The power of the mob, the power of drug lords, the power of corrupt borough machines, and the inertia of the police bureaucracy could only be challenged by another, deeper institutional power.

Unconvinced, unsatisfied, a few people stalked out or didn't return. But the majority of the leaders reluctantly went along. As one leader later said, "Well, we'd tried just about everything else —model cities, poverty programs, causes for this, causes for that. None of it worked. So we didn't have much to lose." Except time. Ed Chambers spent eighteen months working long-distance with the mature and intelligent leaders of what would become East Brooklyn Congregations. They recruited twenty local institutions. They raised, to their complete surprise, nearly $250,000 in dues and grants. They sent hundreds of leaders through local training sessions and fifty through the IAF ten-day training. They ran meetings that started on time and ended on time and lasted one hour. They did all of this work themselves, without a paid staff person, in one of the nation's poorest communities, at the very worst of times, while buildings continued to burn and bullets continued to fly.

This period devoted to building a powerful and durable base —what we in the IAF called the sponsoring committee phase— is what most other organizations, parties, agencies, movements, unions, and civic associations tend to forget, skip, or give short shrift. But it's precisely during these months and years that a community can begin to develop new depth and new breadth, can sort out the majority of hard and persistent workers from the small minority of loudmouths, can tap into talent already present but usually overlooked, and can engage allies and supporters waiting in the wings but not knowing how best to contribute. It's right here, in this gestation phase, that a new culture of public life and public action and clear accountability can begin to form and spread.

In the nearly twenty-three years since, some of the same leaders who sat in a church basement and skeptically eyed the six-foot-five, 250-pound IAF director when he first preached the fundamentals of power organizing have used that power to transform their community. They pressed the city to replace three thousand missing street signs, stop signs, and one-way signs—to put the area, quite literally, back on the map. They negotiated with the parks department to upgrade every park and playground. They leaned on the Transit Authority to renovate the subway and el stations. They made sure that lots were cleaned, streets swept, and drug locations raided. They identified the need for two new primary health centers—and had them built. They pressured the Board of Education to build two new high schools—smaller, safer, more responsive to parent and student needs—and cosponsored them. They increased the registration and turnout of voters, in spite of a series of dreadful and uncompetitive elections. They rekindled a spirit of the possible in a place that had grown dark with cynicism and despair. And—most visibly—they designed and built nearly three thousand new, affordable single-family homes.

An organization with a core budget of three hundred thousand dollars a year, a staff of four, and a modest headquarters in a local apartment complex halted two decades of burning, deterioration, and abandonment by building a critical mass of owner-occupied town houses and generating a chain reaction of other neighborhood improvements. EBC built on every large parcel and abandoned block in the area—140 vacant acres. The market value of the housing built now exceeds $400 million.

The group succeeded in large part because its leaders creatively applied the lessons absorbed during the sponsoring committee phase to the challenge of rebuilding a wasteland with homes affordable to working families making as little as twenty-five thousand dollars a year. Instead of beginning by asking government for funding, the leaders of EBC first raised $8 million of no-interest revolving construction financing from their own church bodies—the Roman Catholic Diocese of Brooklyn, the Episcopal Diocese of Long Island, and the Lutheran Church Missouri Synod. They would never have had the chutzpah to approach their bishops for million-dollar loans if they hadn't decided to pay their own dues and generate their own core budget and discipline themselves to avoid government largesse.

They pushed this principle further. Instead of asking for the most public subsidy available from the City of New York, they asked for the *least* amount of subsidy that any group requested —a no-interest, ten-thousand-dollar-per-home second mortgage with lien. It fact, when the EBC leaders, primarily African American and Hispanic, poor and working poor, approached the city's housing commissioner with their request, he said that he would provide more than they asked for—twenty-five thousand dollars per house to each buyer. A truly bizarre negotiation then ensued, with the EBC leaders demanding less, in the form of a loan, and the city offering more, in the form of a grant. The city officials began to whine, "Why, we give the Rockefeller Partnership housing program twenty-five thousand dollars. How would it look if we gave you less?" This logjam dissolved when the EBC leaders threatened to tell the *New York Times* about this silliness.

Then they pushed it further still. When Ed Chambers and I recommended a down payment of thirty-five hundred dollars on a home then costing fifty thousand dollars, the leaders said no. They voted for a *higher* down payment of five thousand dollars so that they didn't experience a repeat of the dreadful FHA scandal, in which homes were nearly given to families who felt little or no sense of ownership and often treated their properties as if they still belonged to the government, not to them. As a friend of mine said when I told him this story, "They're smart. They're avoiding mental rental."

From the start, these leaders never made the mistake of thinking that the housing program was more important than the power organization. The effort was not viewed as an opportunity to build a large bureaucracy. It wasn't a patronage program. It wasn't an avenue into the profitable world of housing management and consulting contracts. The two general managers hired to do this work—first the incomparable I. D. Robbins, then the astonishingly effective Ron Waters—worked for EBC, not the other way around. They were expected to build homes with a minimum of staff, with modest overhead, and at the lowest possible cost. The EBC Nehemiah effort was seen as an *action of the organization,* a measure of its power, and a test of its ability to pressure, push, and leverage its vision and will against sluggish housing agencies and bankrupt housing theories.

All of this flew in the face of those who fancied themselves experts in housing, urban development, and civic activism, then and now. One political leader said, "You'll never do this. Your eyes are bigger than your stomach." Another said, "Forget it. If you build them, no one will buy them. If they buy them, they won't maintain them." Many housing and foundation executives wondered, aloud, "But who is going to *manage* these people?" Our answer was that they were going to do what all other American home buyers do—manage themselves. We weren't about to do for others what they could do for themselves.

During this same period—nearly a quarter of a century—other groups of leaders in other cities and states were also altering their landscapes. IAF leaders in Baltimore invented and launched the nation's living wage movement. They wrote and passed the first bill requiring municipal contractors to pay their workers a living wage. IAF leaders in Texas applied their power to force cites and states to extend the basic necessities and amenities of modern life, water and sewers and sidewalks, libraries and street signs and playgrounds—to the forgotten corners of San Antonio and Houston and the Rio Grande Valley. They designed and produced the nation's most successful experiment in parent participation and public school improvement—the Alliance Schools Strategy. IAF leaders in Philadelphia imagined a new approach to the reconstruction and revitalization of older, shrinking American cities. IAF leaders in the South Bronx gave birth a new public high school that promises to become the second highest performing school in the borough—right behind the exclusive Bronx High School of Science. These leaders, and thousands like them in other cities and states, have used a combination of power, pressure, and patience to create the conditions that make it possible for people to move from the margins into the social and economic mainstream. They have begun the construction—or reconstruction—of a largely unnoticed

social highway system every bit as important as the nation's inter-
states.

Because these leaders are not protestors, partisans, or helpless
victims but some other and more complicated and very different
thing, they do not fit easily into the media's prewritten stories.
They generate more substance, more production, and more participation than many others, but their names cannot normally be
found in a reporter's Rolodex. They succeed, but they succeed in
unexpected ways and in unexpected places.

This book will describe those ways and visit some of those
places. It will make more public the patterns and habits developed
and tested, through trial and error, by a generation of IAF leaders
and organizers over the past twenty-five years. Each of the four
parts of the book will concentrate on one of these four habits—the
habit of relating, the habit of action, the habit of organizing, and
the habit of reflection.

I'll try to show just how far the steady and disciplined practice
of these habits can transport citizens from the dry and bloodless
formulas of the left and the right, from dusty reports presented in
dull academic symposia, and from meaningless sound bytes and irrelevant exposes manufactured by the media's celebrity industry.
Taken together, these four habits form a new culture of organization accessible to anyone interested in the drama and friction, the
power and the glory, of a fuller and more colorful public life.

PART I

The Habit of Relating

CHAPTER I

All Real Living Is Meeting

In September of 1980, after an eighteen-month period of base building, East Brooklyn Congregations "began." It was a quiet beginning. There was no grand press conference, no ribbon cutting, no march, no promise of spectacular success, no celebrity gushing praise, and no political figures mugging for the cameras. A small team of local leaders met quietly with a newly hired lead organizer, me, to identify other congregations and associations to recruit, to put together a list of other leaders to approach, and to tell me which of the current member congregations would benefit from more intensive local training.

Around this same time, other quiet beginnings were taking place in Texas, where Ernesto Cortes had already created one of the nation's largest citizens organizations, in San Antonio, and was enlisting people like Sr. Christine Stephens, Sr. Pearl Cesar, Elizabeth Valdez, and the late Jim Drake to assist him as he expanded into other southwestern cities. Larry McNeil, a good friend who has just left the IAF, was starting to scratch out the first power organization in southern California. And Arnie Graf was settling into

Baltimore, where he would be joined by Gerald Taylor, now the senior IAF person in the South.

The previous spring, I had spent two days—dreary, wet, cold days—in a side office in Our Lady of Mercy Church on what was then called Stone Avenue. The view from the window of Our Lady of Mercy was uninspiring. A row of abandoned four-story walkups defined the horizon across the street. Windows and doors were long gone. Drug dealers slipped in and out of gangways. Occasionally, later in the day, when the gloom deepened into darkness, light from a match or candle would flicker inside one of the abandoned apartments. Phantom families occupied this broken block.

The leaders chosen by the group to interview me individually—Edgar Mendez, Luella Perez, Alice McCollum, Susanna Lebron, Nellie Hanley, Elda Peralta, and ten others—had watched their community slide into this state over the past twenty years. As I met person after person, hour after hour, I learned that they were embattled, but not beaten. They were stable, solid, and grounded. They treasured their families. They loved their congregations. They trusted their pastors. They all harbored memories of a better time and a better place—whether East Brooklyn thirty years before or a farm in Panama or Puerto Rico. They could still laugh, and often did. They had a steady, workmanlike quality about them. They would never appear in the pages of the *New York Times Magazine,* but they would press forward, under fire, day after day.

Having passed muster, I returned in mid-September to begin as the sole staff person, the lead organizer, of East Brooklyn Congregations. My second meeting on that day in September was with Ed Chambers. We talked awhile and then he handed me a long list of names and phone numbers—seventy-five other leaders from the congregations who made up the beginning base of EBC. "Go get a sense of these leaders," he said, "and let them get a sense of you."

In the middle of worsening deterioration, crime, arson, and abandonment, in a place that looked as if it had been repeatedly bombed and strafed, I resisted the nearly overpowering urge to rush into action and instead filled my schedule with individual meetings. And I began to develop one of the most important habits any leader or organizer can have—the habit of building new public relationships. Power in our society does not just come from the concentration of wealth on Wall Street, the dictates of great governmental agencies, the barrel of a gun, or the fanaticism of a terrorist in the cockpit of a plane. Power can come from the habit of building new public relationships.

The trouble with many of us, and with our culture as whole, is that we don't take the time to "relate," to connect publicly and formally but meaningfully with others. Instead, we live in what Richard Sennett called a "tyranny of intimacy"—presidents pretending to share our pain or talk show hosts prying into the most intimate corners of private life. Or we feel a need to maintain constant and superficial contact with others. We see and are seen by others. We sit in meetings and conferences and dinner sessions with scores and hundreds of others. We "touch base" with others or "make an appearance" or "give brief remarks." We buy and collect better tools—a tyranny of technology—to stay in touch. But all real living is *meeting*, not *meetings*. We don't take the time to meet one to one with others, to hear their interests and dreams and fears, to understand *why* people do what they do or don't do what they don't do.

We forget or deny that the appetite to relate is fundamental, and that the willingness to relate is nearly universal. People who have ideas and drive are on every street, in every project, every workplace and school, waiting in the wings, ready to be discovered. Someone has to reach them and recognize them. Someone has to ask them to step out, not to be consumers or props or spectators but to be players in the unfolding drama of public life. And that someone is what we call a leader or organizer.

One evening, I met Icie Johnson—tall, trim, and regal— a young African-American woman who belonged to St. Paul Community Baptist Church in East New York, where the then-skeptical Johnny Ray Youngblood was pastor. We met one warm evening, with the streets loud and edgy, and I asked her why she wasn't afraid. "I *am* afraid," she said, as she prepared to leave an evening training session and head for the bus stop two blocks away. "I *am* afraid," she repeated. Then why not wait for a ride or call a cab? "Because I'm not fearful," she said. "Not *full* of fear." With that, she headed out into the street. About an hour later, after a training session, I did too. And, in a sense, I've been following Icie Johnson ever since.

These leaders were already forged and mature in many ways. They understood in their bones the need for accountability and internal discipline—lessons learned from their lives as leaders in their religious institutions. They accepted tension, conflict, and confrontation as facts of life and the price of progress—perhaps from their own tough encounters on forbidding streets or maybe from raising children and nurturing families among fields filled with rubble.

They knew they had enemies but did not hate them. They weren't distracted by the media, in part because the media found no reason to solicit their views. They had no community reputation to defend or promote because, unlike the South Bronx or Harlem, mayors and presidents rarely visited. They were wary of outsiders—especially white outsiders like Ed and myself—but were willing to give us the benefit of the doubt, at least, for a while. They were sophisticated in ways that the swells on Park Avenue could scarcely imagine.

In my first months in East Brooklyn, I began to wonder what I had gotten myself into. I would call leaders for individual meetings, and several would offer to meet me at my office, rather than have me come to their homes or apartments. "Too dangerous," Domingo Lind said one afternoon. "Can't be that dangerous," I countered. We compromised. He asked me to call when I was about to come over. He would head down from his twelfth-floor apartment and meet me in the lobby of his project. When I arrived about fifty young guys were milling around the courtyard and lobby—the same fifty or more guys who "owned" that space every day and every night. Mr. Lind spotted my car and walked toward me as I parked. The guys who were already heading my way backed off just a bit. He ushered me through a cordon of hostile eyes, into the elevator, up to his tidy apartment, where he served us both coffee, and I asked him how the hell he survived. He took me down the elevator and back to the car after our session—the same drill he did at midnight when his wife walked home from the subway and in the morning and afternoon when his kids went to and from school. He wasn't a particularly big or tough-looking man. He didn't carry a gun or knife. He was afraid but was not full of fear. The faith and courage and determination that he displayed to the toughs in the lobby and courtyard created just enough space to live a life. In his twelfth-floor apartment, over coffee, for thirty minutes, he told me what that life consisted of—his work, his role in his church, his dreams for his children, and his attempts to improve his project. And I learned that Domingo Lind was a leader.

A few nights later, as I headed onto the Interboro (now the Jackie Robinson Parkway), guns flashed on either side of the road. Gangs were battling it out at nine at night. I ducked—ducked!—as if somehow that would help me get through.

In the winter, late one night, again on the Interboro, two cars had been upended on either side of the road and had been torched. The shadows of young men danced on the trunks of the trees. The map said Brooklyn. The mind said Vietnam. Like Icie Johnson and Domingo Lind, I was afraid much of the time—still am—but not so full of fear that I couldn't function as an organizer.

One night, a year or so later, I was knocking on the door of Mt. Ararat Baptist Church, in Oceanhill. Mt. Ararat, then, was one of the few occupied buildings in a blighted landscape. Across Howard Avenue was a long-abandoned school. Down each block were vacant lots and abandoned homes. No one lived nearby, so the streets were desolate. Mt. Ararat somehow held on, on the high ground, led by a gentle giant named James T. Reeder.

I knocked and knocked, a little unnerved by the moonscape around me. To my left, three young men sauntered toward me. When they reached me, they stopped. I turned to face them.

"You the pastor?" One of them said.

"No." I said, praying for Reverend Reeder to appear.

"You own this building?"

"No."

"You a cop?"

I paused. "You can stop right there."

My questioner smiled. He looked at his buddies. "Told you" was all he said, as they walked away, nodding knowingly.

By the time Reverend Reeder unbolted the door and opened it, I was almost too tired to meet with him. But he proved to be worth the wait and the risk.

When you develop the habit of doing individual meetings, you stop thinking of people as "the poor" or the "the rich" or "the establishment" or even "the enemy." You don't just size up another person to see if you can make a sale—whether the commodity is the church, the doctrine, the political candidate, or the citizens organization that you happen to be packaging and marketing that day. You resist the urge to find out just enough about Icie Johnson, Domingo Lind, or James T. Reeder to determine whether or not they will follow you or "plug into" your worldview or your set of assumptions.

No, you sit and listen, you probe and challenge. You try to gauge whether or not you and the other can build the kind of public relationship that is mutual and respectful and capable of withstanding the tension that all healthy relating tends to generate over time. You challenge them in a way that you can only do effectively when you are face to face, one to one, "How can you stand to live in this place? What have you tried to do to turn it around? Are you willing to work with groups you say you dislike to make a difference here?" And you let others agitate you, as they did. "What are you, a white guy, doing here?" "What makes you think that EBC will be any different from all the other do-nothing groups around here?" "What does any of this have to do with ministry and faith, anyway?"

Done well, individual meetings allow people to break out of the kinds of relational ruts that limit us all. The person who walks in the door of the congregation is no longer just a congregant or client. And the person who works on the parish staff ceases being a one-dimensional provider. We see more of the many facets of people who have come to think of themselves as invisible or voiceless not just because the powers that be fail to see them and hear them, but because those who claim to care about their concerns also fail to relate to them and with them. And they see more facets of you. They see a not particularly big, not particularly tough, not particularly gung-ho person standing in their doorway—someone with real questions, not a set of slick answers, someone with a feel for politics, not a simple formula, someone who can laugh and who can fight, if need be.

Wherever I went in a neighborhood that one pastor called "a graveyard," I found vital, able, complicated people. They had an appetite for learning, for relating across the lines of race and culture, and eventually for acting in new and effective ways. The number of individual meetings multiplied as I began to teach the leaders to schedule them—and then multiplied even more when I hired Stephen Roberson to work as my associate. This tall, unflappable veteran of the United Farm Workers traded his beret and blue jeans for a sport coat and tie and dove into the growing number of congregations that made up the organization.

We all ranged beyond the borders of East Brooklyn to meet leaders in other arenas. It was important to hear how other New Yorkers saw the world. And it was important for other New Yorkers to meet leaders from East Brooklyn who didn't look or sound or act anything like the cartoon characters portrayed by most of the media. Not long after I began, at the suggestion of several local pastors, I sought a meeting with the head of the Roman Catholic Diocese of Brooklyn and Queens, Bishop Francis J. Mugavero. Some of those who thought they knew the bishop, who passed away in 1991, said in 1980 that he was near the end of his career, that he was out of favor with the Vatican, that he had run the diocese into financial difficulties and was coasting toward retirement.

When I arrived at the bishop's office, he greeted me warmly. His office was across the street from Bishop Loughlin High School, the alma mater of my father-in-law and several generations of Roman Catholic cops and pols, FBI agents and U.S. attorneys. It served as one of the great training grounds for Catholic kids moving from poverty or the working class into middle- and upper-middle-class life.

The bishop was short, bald, soft-spoken, straightforward, irreverently funny, and about as far from retirement as any sixty-five-year-old man I have ever met. He embodied the best qualities of millions of European immigrants who had put one foot on American shores just decades before and now had both feet planted squarely in the center of their cities and their nation. He reminded me of the men from my old neighborhood—the men I used to watch with awe from a booth in my parents' bar, the hard-working railroad workers who had shots of vo and bottles of Schlitz with the sandwiches and soup my mother prepared in our tavern's kitchen before they returned for five more hours of hard labor repairing track.

My goal was to get my own sense of him and to give him a sense of me. I hoped that he would refer me to others in the city he thought I should meet with. Given all that I had heard about him I was more than a little surprised to find a man looking for new and interesting things to do. He was "political" in the way Monsignor Jack Egan in Chicago was—curious about how the public world worked, wanting to learn how he could make more of an impact there, hungry for tidbits of gossip or new insights and stories, happy to hear about the craziness and complexity of life in New York and ready to mix it up again in the public arena. Here's another reason why it's so important to do individual meetings: sometimes, in fact fairly often, you will find that people bear almost no resemblance to the image others have of them or the public presentation that they and their spin doctors manufacture.

He was called "Mugsy" by his friends—a nickname that accurately captured his openness and informality. I never called him that, of course, in spite of the fact that we met scores of times over the ten years we worked closely together, that we negotiated agreements with the city together, that we sweated out terrible crises and spent many tense nights sorting out our situation with mayors and other officials and plotting the next day's battle plans.

He was interested in everything—the state of his inner-city parishes, the well-being of his priests, the future of the city, even the fact that I was asking him for references, for other people to meet with. "What for?" he asked. "For *this*, Bishop," I said, "so that I can get a sense of other interesting leaders in the city and they can get a sense of me and our work. I'd like to get the lay of the land, so that, when we act, we don't act in a vacuum and we don't act alone."

He gave me a number of names and said that I could use him as a reference. Then, as I was leaving, he added one more, "Go see Mario Cuomo—and tell me what you think of him."

At the time, Mario Cuomo was the lieutenant governor of New York, a largely ceremonial and powerless position. He had been a local civic leader who had made a name for himself by serving as the attorney to vulnerable homeowners in the Corona section of Queens. He was Queens and Catholic to the core in those days, always ready to regale an audience about his upbringing in St. Monica's Parish in Jamaica.

I called for an appointment—an anonymous organizer, new to the city, seeking a meeting with a well-known state official—and got one almost immediately because the bishop allowed me to use his name. When I arrived at his World Trade Center office, Cuomo was on time, welcoming, but fairly fidgety. He listened for sixty seconds or so to my introduction of myself—EBC, the Industrial Areas Foundation, Saul Alinsky, and so on. When I mentioned Alinsky's name, he quoted one of Alinsky's sayings, talked a bit about his own experience in Corona, and said that he had concluded that there were limits to this kind of organizing. I didn't argue, said there were limits to every option, and then asked him why he had decided to pursue the path in public life that led from local activism to public office. By now, perhaps four minutes into the session, he was growing very impatient.

"What do you really want?" he asked. Well, nothing immediate today, I said, I'm in the early stages of getting to know the situation in New York, in Brooklyn . . .

Before I could finish the sentence, he hit a button on the phone to his right. A side door opened, almost immediately, and two aides rushed in. "These," Cuomo declared, "are my Brooklyn people. Tell them what you want."

The two aides sat down and opened notebooks. Taken aback a bit, I said to Cuomo, "I don't *want* anything—other than to hear how you see the state of the city . . . ." He wasn't having any of it.

"You're the one who said 'Brooklyn.' These are my Brooklyn people. Now tell them what you want."

"What I *wanted* was a half-hour of your time to get a sense of how you see things . . . ." I knew I was finished. Cuomo was still sitting there but had mentally ended the meeting. I mumbled a few things to the staff and left after a few more minutes. I learned more about myself and how not to approach a person like Cuomo. But I also learned a fair amount about him. Far from being thoughtful, sensitive, and ruminative, as he had been described to me, he was brusque, reactive, and devoid of curiosity. In future encounters, when our leaders did want to talk about specific matters, we made sure to present the important issues early in the meetings, in the very short time before his attention span snapped and aides swarmed in.

The best and most effective organizing—in schools, in corporations, in unions, in congregations, in politics, anywhere—still starts when people rediscover the habit of doing individual meetings well and then consistently do them. The right public relationship, as a major bank claims in its advertising, *is* everything.

As a result of these right relationships, in these face-to-face encounters, in the form of confrontation (from the Latin "con" and "frons," foreheads together) that we should be famous for, new leaders and issues begin to emerge. For example, some years ago, in Baltimore, a Baptist pastor decided to take the time to sit down and meet individually with people who came to his church for a free lunch each day. The pastor noticed a decently dressed young man and sat across from him. The pastor asked, after some initial back and forth, "Why don't you have a job?" The man responded, "But I do have a job." Then the pastor probed, "Then why are you here?" And the man said, "Because I don't make nearly enough money to afford to eat."

So this mildly astonished pastor listened over lunch to a story of America in the 1990s—a place where men and women could work full-time, as temporary workers, at minimum wage, with no benefits and no time off, and not be able to afford food, phone service, heat, and clothes for themselves and their families. The pastor then made it a habit to sit down with someone each day at lunch. And the people on the line ceased being clients of the congregation's soup kitchen. They became names, histories, faiths, and tragedies—full and complex human beings, with sometimes beautiful and sometimes painful and sometimes frustrating stories.

The pastor enlisted the help of Jonathon Lange, the BUILD lead organizer, who had come to the IAF to apply what he had learned as a union organizer to the field of citizens organizing and to absorb lessons from citizens organizing that he could translate into the more effective organizing of workers. Jonathon, his staff, and other leaders did hundreds of individual meetings in settings like the soup kitchen, on street corners in downtown Baltimore where the workers gathered to catch the bus after stints as janitors in office buildings or hotels or Camden Yards, and in local fast-food restaurants where weary workers gathered for a quick snack or cup of coffee.

Out of these rapidly multiplying individual meetings, a fuller picture of the day-to-day lives of these workers developed, and leaders emerged. Men and women who could not afford telephones, who sometimes went home to darkened apartments because of unpaid utility bills, who moved from relative to relative with children in tow to minimize housing costs, who lived a shadow life in a shadow city, designed the nation's first living wage campaign, authored and passed the nation's first living wage law, built the first low-wage workers' organization, and started the first living wage job agency for the working poor.

The pastor in the soup kitchen rediscovered the tool called the individual meeting and then disciplined himself to use that tool day after day. Sitting across the lunchroom table from the good citizens of Baltimore, he was reviving and extending an American tradition.

Imagine John Adams and his long rides from Massachusetts to and from Philadelphia. He often traveled with just one companion. He spent days on the road, encountering people in taverns and stables. When he wasn't speaking one to one or in small groups to fellow Americans, he was communicating one to one through letters, hundreds of letters, to his friends and family and colleagues. The demands of travel by horseback were offset by the countless hours free of beepers, cell phones, and e-mail that he spent reading poetry and thinking, actually thinking.

Remember Lincoln, who rode for years from small town to small town as a local lawyer and anonymous state legislator. He sat outside general stores and met individually with people. He doggedly built relationships over many miles and many years. Our democracy was founded and forged by women and men who were quirky and complex, but profoundly relational. It may be that the very habit of building public relationships is part of the human constitution of a vital democracy, just as the habit of thinking and reflecting is fundamental to our ability to make ethical and moral choices.

Consider my father. August Gecan, a Croatian teenager, immigrated to Chicago in the thirties. The pastor of the local Catholic church in his new Chicago neighborhood, Holy Trinity Parish on

18th and Throop Street, stopped by to visit him and did an individual meeting with him. Then, nearly every year of my father's life, for a span of sixty years, that pastor and the pastor who succeeded him when the first pastor died, and the pastor after that, took the time to do an individual meeting with my father. It didn't matter that my father did not consider himself "special." Was not a professional. Was not rich. Was not a big giver. Was not a model parishioner. Moved away from the parish when he married. Then moved again, and again. Each year, the priest visited. And each year my father was honored to have him visit. And, until the day of his death, he maintained his ties to that parish and that community and those priests.

In a culture of quick encounters and multiple contacts, of instant access and empty photo-ops, there are fewer and fewer public relationships of this depth and quality. The absence of these relationships creates great gaps in our society—where alienated people become more detached, where lost and damaged people spin further out of control, where the apathetic and the enraged drift further away from a human center, where killers and terrorists hide in plain sight, shopping at the supermarket, drinking at the bar. We will never have enough technology or enough security officers or social workers or government programs to compensate for the loss or thinning of public relationships.

But we don't *need* an expensive PalmPilot, an MBA, or a costly business suit to learn the art of the individual meeting and to develop the habit of doing them. We just need the clarity, the confidence, and the time—and the support of others who understand what is fundamental to effective organizing and constructive leadership and what is peripheral and inessential.

CHAPTER 2

The World as It Is

O f course, you don't build relationships in a vacuum. The world outside the door of the church always influences your actions, options, and possibilities. Thugs still control some corners. Gangsters still shake down your construction site. Local politicians with little power and less ability divert and distract you. The market rewards some and punishes many. The unskilled wander through a half-work-life while a celebrity culture creates expensive new needs. Institutions shift and drift, responsible at times, damaging at times. And we shift and drift, responsible at times, not at times. King George wants you dead. The South has seceded and engaged in a war of numbing destruction. Community "activists" shout outrageous comments at the media and claim to speak for "the people." Terrorists strike—the terrorist in the housing project elevator late at night, the terrorists in the jets that dive out of the morning sky. The world, on a good day, is like the inside of City Hall at the height of the Koch years—crowded, loud, raucous, confusing, and even dangerous.

So, you are building relationships in a tough and noisy world, and you must find the time to talk with the people you meet individually about the very nature of that world and the need for a new public identity. And you must do it on the ground, literally where people live, in the limited time that they can carve out of their already-packed schedules, in the precious hours they pry from work, family, and congregation. You must add the habit of training and reflection to the habit of individual meetings. And you must do this, not in the quiet confines of the Woodrow Wilson School at Princeton but in the basements and classrooms of neighborhoods and cities that often feel under siege.

Let me take you to one of those sessions on a typical night in East Brooklyn. Just before seven, the leaders file in—twenty-two people, mostly African American, mostly in their forties and fifties, mostly coming straight from the subway or bus stop after long days on their jobs. They have signed up for six hours of training —two hours a night for three straight nights—on the topics of power, leadership, and action.

I start with the rounds, by asking people who they are, where they are from, and what their expectations are for the training tonight. About half of the group is from Pastor Youngblood's St. Paul Community Baptist—the church that makes the best and fullest use of every aspect of our organizing. What Pastor Youngblood's people know is that he will invest in their growth and development by sending them to almost any workshop that will improve their leadership skills, their educational level, their nutritional habits, and their spiritual life. He is not afraid that they will learn more. He is concerned that they will not be exposed to enough opportunity. He is not worried that they will outgrow him. No, in many ways, every day, he communicates to them that he believes that it is his duty as pastor and their duty as members to grow and develop as quickly and as fully as possible. And they love him for it. They describe how they want to be more effective as leaders in their church, running their societies, finding new members, and identifying and training others. Two other leaders, from a small, struggling Lutheran church, want to learn how they can help save and then expand their congregation. Another seven people come from homeowners associations and parents groups looking for additional skills and tools to improve their groups.

After the rounds, I begin by writing "the world as it is" on the left side of the board—blue marker on white surface—and "the world as it should be" on the right. I draw a dotted line between the two phrases and write the word "tension" below it. The entire session is going to focus on the challenge of operating effectively in the world as it is, where power is the prime moving force, and trying to keep that world and that power in tension with the loftier values of the world as it should be.

Even here, next to the elevated trains of the Broadway Junction station, on a freezing night in Brooklyn, in an old factory that is now a new school, even among people who have spent their entire lives in some of the roughest corners of the world as it is, among men and women who carry the scars of their lives on their faces, there is a profound puzzlement.

Teachers should teach, they say. Politicians should represent their communities, they insist. Mayors should do the right things for the right reasons, they claim. Cops should treat them with respect, and banks should give them the same terms and the same access as they offer others. Should . . . should . . . should—there's frustration in the voices now.

I tell them what all my experience has taught me, what Ed Chambers, Arnie Graf, Christine Stephens, and Stephen Roberson have found as well: you can't get near what *should* be, not even close, unless you build and use power, unless you manipulate that power so that you can slog through the mud of the world as it *is*, unless you are willing to push and tug the teachers and mayors and pols and cops and yourself and your own institutions in the direction of what ought to be.

There's that word—"POWER"—in large letters. I write it directly under the heading of the world as it is. Without power, there's no real recognition. They don't even see you. They never learn your name. Without recognition, there's no reciprocity; there's not even a "you" to respond to. And without reciprocity, there's no real relationship of respect. Without power, you can only be a supplicant, a serf, a victim, or a wishful thinker who soon begins to whine. Power in the new millennium is the same as power when Thucydides was writing about the Melians and the Athenians. It is still the ability to act. And it still comes in two basic forms—organized people and organized money. And you still need it to function in the public arena.

A vocal man on my left—fifty-five, aggressive, bright—is agitated and argues hard. "Then what do we pay them for?" "Who?" I ask. "The teachers and police, the politicians and others. What do we pay them for?"

"You pay them to do what they are hired to do," I say, "but you still have to have the power to make them do it if they won't."

"I don't agree with this. This is not right."

"It's not a question of right or wrong. It's a question of what is, what reality is, and what happens to you when you meet this reality."

Others in the room are debating, some taking my side, some taking his.

A woman who hasn't said a word all night chimes in, "It should not be this way."

"Of course not," I say. "But if you just keep saying that, and you just keep waiting for it to change, without any power, you become sour and detached. Most people do the right thing, if they do it, for the wrong reason, or for mixed reasons. That's the way it is—not just for those 'out there' beyond these walls—but even for those of us who think our motives are fine and our hearts are pure. We're like 'them.' We need people in our lives who have the power to hold us accountable, to pressure us at times, to check us at times, and to stop us at times. Just like 'they' need organized people like us."

How do you think new and better schools will be built? Because they are desperately needed? Because it's a good idea? Because the honchos at the Board of Education wake up in the morning and decide to do the right thing? Because the city is appalled by the chronic overcrowding? No, new and better schools will be built when you have the power to force them to build them.

How do you think the new Nehemiah homes—*your new Nehemiah homes*—were built? Automatically? Because you all are wonderful and hardworking people who deserve the same opportunities as other racial and ethnic groups? Because it's the right thing? No, same answer. The right kind of housing will rise here when you have enough power to insist that it be built. Not before then. You're going to have to have enough organized people and enough organized money, enough discipline and enough luck, to *make it happen*. That's the way it works in the world as it is.

Even though I have had my own experiences in the world, have seen disaster and death, have lived in a tough and violent place, have fought for my life many times in my youth, I recognize the irony of my standing before these twenty-two leaders, all now living a much harsher life than mine, and agitating them to come to grips with the nature of the world as it is.

I end the evening by trying to teach an unusual lesson in identity. You can build new relationships with talented people. And you can shake up their views of the world as it is. You can posit the reality and necessity of power. But, then, people can rush right out the door and get creamed again—unless they understand who they are and where they are.

In the world as it should be, I say, we are each individuals, with our individual views and interests, our individual talents and limitations, respected and equal. The rich and the powerful, products of the best of society's institutions and beneficiaries of many overlapping institutional supports, often believe this myth, believe that others listen to them and respond to them because of the brilliance of their wit or the force of their will—not the wealth in their wallets. People without wealth and power, the vast majority of people, can't operate in the public arena if they regard themselves as detached individuals or if they just search for the right words, clothes, or degrees to help them get by.

I say that there is no "Mike Gecan, individual" in the public arena. That person doesn't exist. I don't think of myself that way. I don't believe that journalists, corporate leaders, or political figures relate and respond to the singular, wonderful me. No, they relate to me, to the extent that they do, often grudgingly, because they understand the "corporate me"—the "me" that has relationships with leaders like Reverend Johnny Ray Youngblood and Betty Turner, Irving Domenech and Maria Nieves. And that's how I think of myself, whether I'm at City Hall, the *Times* editorial board, or the Chamber of Commerce.

Now, most of the time, this is relatively easy, even obvious, because I am almost always *with* others in all of these settings. But even when I'm not, even when I am alone in the public arena, I am not an individual. To forget this would be to become, quite literally, in the Greek sense, an idiot. Robert Penn Warren once wrote of the "murderous innocence of the American people." Trying to operate in the world as it is as a worthy but powerless individual is suicidal innocence.

I learned this lesson in a most unusual place, in a most unusual way—in Gracie Mansion, in the middle of Ed Koch's troubled third term. Our Queens affiliate, the Queens Citizens Organization, had proposed to build thousands of Nehemiah homes in the

Rockaways, and the same mayor who sometimes refers to himself as one of the earliest supporters of the Brooklyn Nehemiah effort had fought us every step of the way.

One morning, the administrator in the Brooklyn office, Lucille Clark, took a call from the mayor's appointments director. The mayor was inviting my wife and me to dinner at Gracie Mansion in three weeks. When Lucille reached me, I asked her to call the number back and see if this was some kind of hoax. I have several warped friends who think this kind of thing might be funny. No, the number was in fact picked up by someone at City Hall. The appointments person answered. Lucille asked her what the agenda for the night was. The appointments person said, "Dinner." Lucille asked who else has been invited. The appointments person said, "We don't give out that information."

Every fiber in my system screamed, "Don't Go." The only hesitation centered on the slim chance that the mayor may have wanted, in his own way, to suggest a compromise solution to the Rockaways battle, perhaps a portion of the site for us and a larger portion for market builders, perhaps an alternative site in another part of Queens. I remembered who I was—politically—and asked the strategy teams of our three New York efforts to consider whether we should accept this invitation. I went so far as to ask each team to vote on it. They all thought it was worth a shot. Then I called Bishop Mugavero and asked for his advice and blessing. He didn't know what to make of it either, but he said, wisely, "If you *don't* go, he'll have one on you, on us, so just for that reason, you probably should go."

I sat down with my supervisor, Ed Chambers, and talked it over. He had even less faith in this than I did but finally advised me to accept the invitation. I'll never forget the last piece of instruction he gave me as I left his office. "Just remember, Mike, the door swings both ways. You can always leave."

Then I talked it over with my wife, a fourth-generation New

Yorker, who said, "As much as I would love to see the inside of Gracie Mansion, I'm not going. This will be all business, at best. I'll keep a hamburger on the side for you just in case."

All this consultation took place over a few days—all made possible by years of working relationships and deep reservoirs of mutual respect and trust among those involved.

On the appointed night, I—not the singular me, but the organizational person who was accountable and connected to three teams of leaders, a Roman Catholic Bishop, the IAF director, and scores of thousands of members of our local groups—parked my car a few blocks from Gracie Mansion and walked over. Koch was running late to his own dinner party, so I found myself sitting in a plush chair, in a lovely room, with an interesting group—a Holocaust scholar, a founder of a residence for runaway teens, a manufacturer of firearms and longtime Koch confidant, a director of a social service program, and a journalist. After a few minutes, Koch rushed in with the last two guests—the Marriotts, the hotel people, fresh off a plane from Salt Lake City.

Koch settled in and asked everyone to introduce themselves. Around we went, with everyone saying who they were and what they did and Koch asking good leading questions. When the introductions got to me—and I was last, sitting next to the mayor—I began. Koch interrupted me immediately. "No, no, no, let me introduce you." He said a few sentences about the agitator Saul Alinsky and then asked me, "Now, tell us, how far to the left of Chairman Mao is the Alinsky group?" He was trying to be funny, but no one was laughing. Then Koch launched into a long story about his first encounter with our Queens organization—comparing the assembly of one thousand leaders to the Moscow show trials and a Nuremberg rally. Midway into his recitation, all given with verve, I interrupted him. "I'm going to need to say something about this when you finish."

"Oh, don't worry, you'll have time for rebuttal," he said, and then talked on. My fellow guests, to their credit, looked pained, or shocked, or uncomfortable, particularly Mrs. Marriott. What could she have been thinking? That I was these things Koch was implying, in which case what was she doing here? Or that I wasn't—and Koch was cruel and a little crazy.

When he stopped, I could barely speak. I said to the rest of the group, "The only problem with the mayor's story is that there is not a fact in it." Then I tried to describe the moderates who make up our best organizations. The gun maker, who had sat through scores of dinners and seen this routine many times before, tried to be solicitous, asked a few good questions, and praised our work.

But it was too late. I knew that I couldn't eat this mayor's food after what he had done. But I also knew that I had to try to teach him a lesson. So I waited a few minutes, until the mayor banged the arm of his chair and urged all of us toward the dining room. As everyone filed in, I stayed back and asked for a word with him. He and I stared at one another, face to face, alone.

"I won't be eating dinner with you tonight," I said.

"Oh," he said, "I've offended you. I see that you're upset. I apologize."

"You *apologize?*"

"Yes, sincerely, I didn't mean to offend you . . ."

"You offended me and everyone I work with. You compared us to Communists and Nazis in the same breath. You smeared us in front of perfect strangers . . ."

"I really do apologize," he began, nervous now, sweating a bit. The doorways to the room filled with the maids and waiters who worked at Gracie Mansion—all minority, all curious, all intent on the drama playing out in the sitting room.

"I'm leaving. Where's my coat?" I said—and it struck me then how awkward it would be for the mayor to go into his dining room and sit at the head of his table and explain why I wouldn't be filling the empty seat reserved there for me. I kept repeating Ed Chambers's last lines to myself.

The mayor took the lapels of my suit and held them. He pulled me closer to him and said, "You can't do this. You can't do this to me."

"My coat . . ."

"You can't . . ."

"The hell with it. You can keep my coat," I said, and broke away from him and headed for the door.

"No," he cried. "I'll get your coat!" Which he did. I didn't stop to put it on. Just went for the door and gave it a good slam. I walked for thirty minutes up and down the streets of the Upper East Side—angry, fuming, wondering if I had done the right thing. When I had settled down enough, I went home to my family and a hamburger.

The next morning, the mayor began calling my office long before I arrived. I didn't take the call. By noon, a two-page letter of apology had arrived, inviting me to return another time, with my spouse. I never responded, knowing that he would wonder whom I would tell the story to and whether it would someday appear in print.

The leaders in the training session enjoy hearing the story, almost as much as I enjoy telling it.

So it is, I say, that the more public relationships you have with leaders and potential leaders, the more you see yourself as part of a larger relational whole, the more you will be able to project your voice and promote your interests when you step into the public arena, and the more clearly will you be able to judge when to sit and sip your drink and when to get up and go.

Two hours fly by. At nine, on the dot, the session ends, as advertised. The leaders are still buzzing as they walk out of the room. People seem less tired that when the training began.

Some people understand the need to have a corporate identity in the public arena. They know that it is critical to operate with others, to create an organization in this world of organizations and institutions. Yet they remain unclear about how to use that identity with strength. The corporate ego is there but not muscular enough to create the kind of impression or impact that matters.

This becomes apparent in a training session I do with a group of forty-five senior citizen leaders in New York. These leaders are a delight—diverse in every way but age and completely full of vinegar. It's one of the few organizations where poor, working class, and middle class, Christians and Jews, women and men of all races find themselves with the same challenges, the same limitations, and the same concerns. They all want lower-cost prescription drugs and more access to housing that they can afford and less lip service from national and local candidates.

The animating spirit of this group belongs to Shirley Genn—a Jewish woman with a long history as a politically active educator in the New York Public Schools system. She was progressive in the fifties and sixties, when that word meant so much more than it does today, and she considered herself an organizer when the role carried with it more weight and much risk.

Mrs. Genn has asked me to work with her leaders to prepare them for their yearly trip to Albany. These visits have grown increasingly predictable and frustrating—a long bus ride to a grim capital city, for a few short meetings with the junior aides of eccentric and pompous legislators, and then a tired ride home.

The very youthful aides, in training for careers in political arrogance, often keep the seniors waiting. When the delayed meetings do begin, the aides often take phone calls or leave the room for hushed discussions with still-more-junior staffers. The culture of contempt for active citizenry is nearly universal—taught, learned, practiced, and perfected by everyone in the legislative establishment from the governor to the newest receptionist.

I take the time to describe the world as it really is in Albany. Most of the legislators need not even be there, except for a few ratification votes. Three men—the governor, Senate leader, and Assembly speaker—make every major decision and dictate to the followers in their respective parties how to vote. The more irrelevant the rest of the legislative apparatus is, the more it tries to prove to the world that it is important, the harder it is to approach, the more grudging it is with its time and attention, and the thicker and more numerous are the veils it drapes between itself and the public.

I describe this reality and then work with the seniors on how to "talk" to the three men who really count and how to avoid those you don't. I tell story after story, most of them funny, about this world, which I have learned about directly and through those who were a part of it or who have learned to navigate it. The seniors in the room are both entertained and dismayed. They often disagree and assert that this is not the way it ought to be, not the way it should be, not what they were told or taught.

One very elderly woman, exasperated, fuming, slowly stands. The other seniors notice her and grow silent. She points a finger at me and nearly yells, "Where were you ten years ago? You could have saved us so much time!"

At the end of the tumultuous session, which feels more like a scrimmage with these vocal and argumentative seniors, I write in large letters on the board, "Things to avoid."

First, I write, "Avoid most low-level staff." All that they can do is take notes, which their mid-level staff will never read and their legislative bosses will never see. It's better to meet with no one, better to go to lunch, shop, or head to the art museum, than to meet with a scribe whose self-importance is affirmed when good citizens travel hundreds of miles for a few precious minutes of his or her time.

Second, I write, "Avoid asking for no-cost commitments." In

every legislature, there are issues that politicians can commit to. But the commitment is meaningless because the legislator knows that the bill will never pass, usually because of the majority opposition of the other party. So, when a group asks for support of a bill that will never have a prayer of passing, the legislator can readily agree, appear responsive, and never lift a finger. When the group asks for another form of support that may involve work or a real trade-off, he can always say that he supported the group on the earlier issue, that the group should be appreciative, and that he can't support the seniors on every matter. His commitment has cost him nothing, in fact has created a rationale for him to resist requests that would cost him time or energy or political capital on other matters.

Third, I print in large letters, "Avoid pats on the head." Elected officials often compete with one another to look as if they are champions of the needs of elderly. They recognize the latent power, the potentially punishing power, of seniors as a group. But often, when these elected officials attend meetings or luncheons organized by the seniors, they refer to them as "my seniors." They hug and kiss and call the seniors by their first names. They call the chairperson Mamie or Tony, even though they have never met Mrs. Orlando or Mr. Ramirez before and will not give them the time of day two months later in Albany.

"My seniors"—I say it with contempt. The seniors shift in their chairs. The room grows quiet and tense. I tell them it's like saying "my pets," "my puppets," or "my begonias." Don't put up with these meaningless gestures and insulting comments. Demand the respect that you've earned and deserve. Be bigger. Think bigger. Act bigger.

Some of the seniors laugh nervously, but others are uneasy, agitated, or quietly reflective. There's no agreement, much less consensus, just a roomful of citizens talking among themselves about the basic questions and tactical tips that we've discussed. And that's where most of our best training ends—leaving people stirred up, examining their habits in the public arena, imagining themselves operating in a different way, and fitter for the vital democratic duties that lie before them.

One of those democratic duties we prepare people for is direct public action.

PART II

The Habit of Action

CHAPTER 3

Activists on a
Manhattan Street

O n a lovely May morning in Manhattan two years ago, I hus-
tled from the PATH station below the World Trade Center (it
still smolders as I write these words, on a Saturday in late September) and headed down Trinity Place to an office I worked in a block
away. It was a busy, crowded, normal day, except for one thing.
Police were stationed everywhere—hundreds of officers, scores of
cars, and a mobile command center in the Trade Center's plaza, all
the signs of a major security operation.

A Hispanic officer stood next to one of the concrete flowerpots
that doubled as a barrier outside the southeast tower of the complex—one of scores that circled the center since the terrorist
bombing in 1993. I asked him what was up.

"Seattle demonstrators," he sniffed. "They got some kind of
chapter here. They think they're gonna do something today . . . ."
He didn't seem overly concerned. His black carrying pack was half
hidden in the foliage in the flowerpot. Behind each planter stood
an officer at his station. Clusters of cops congregated near the intersections. Police brass with names and ranks prominently dis-

played on their shirts or jackets circulated along Church Street. The cop tells me that they have all been in place since dawn. The demonstration isn't scheduled to start until three or so.

At noon, when I left my office and looked for lunch, a small "action" was under way. Five people stood at the corner of Broadway and Rector Street. Two had splashed black paint on their clothing and smeared black paint on their faces. They writhed on the sidewalk while a graying demonstrator pounded a drum and a young woman harangued the passing crowd. Twenty-five cops eyed the scene, casually leaning against buildings and stairs, their nightsticks in their belts, their riot helmets perched on their nightsticks.

It was a spectacular afternoon—bright and mild—and the entire spectacle seemed to move slowly, languidly. Actors, officers, observers—no one appeared to be fully engaged. I walked over to a local Starbucks, only to find it closed, with yellow police tape roping off its front entrance. In the middle of the night, someone had hurled a hammer through the window. In Seattle Starbucks facilities had been the target of extensive vandalism. It's a poor choice, I thought, more likely to turn coffee lovers away from the demonstrators than to attract new recruits to their cause.

But what *was* their cause?

The demonstrators held a hastily painted sing: "Save the U'Wa Tribe . . ." There was a reference to Fidelity Capital. The woman with the megaphone couldn't be easily understood. An aging fellow demonstrator banged a drum. Meanwhile, the two paint-splattered figures on the sidewalk continued to contort. For all their choreographed movement, the demonstrators seemed remarkably static. Still life: *Activists on a Manhattan Street.*

Often, as I start a training session or a talk, I ask people to describe the last public action—large or small—they participated in. I give the broadest and most basic definition of an action: it's when more than one person, focused on a specific issue, engages a person in power directly responsible for that issue, for the purpose of getting a reaction. Twenty seniors meeting with a powerful politician about the cost of prescription drugs is an action. Eight parents pressing the local school principal to improve pedestrian safety around the local school is an action. Three thousand leaders meeting with the mayor of Baltimore demanding that the city pay living wages is an action. After posing my question, I watch people grow silent and begin to ponder. They usually need to reach all the way back to the late sixties or early seventies to come up with an answer. They sometimes confess that they have never participated in an action.

Some people believe that action is passé—like wearing bell-bottoms or displaying a peace sign. Or it may strike people as terrifying and appalling—the kind of action taken by the terrorists who murdered the innocent workers of the World Trade Center or the action of a criminal standing right behind you on the long ride down in the elevator of a housing project late at night: Action is something to outgrow, to avoid, and to defend yourself against.

Others look for substitutes or alternatives to action. They join advocacy groups and write charitable checks. They attend conferences, discussion clubs, and workshops about crises or issues —AIDS, racial tensions, school construction costs, immigration, sprawl. They watch the evening news, CNN, or MSNBC, and in-depth programs about the conditions in our cities or other countries. They surf the Net and chat with those who share their views. But none of this is action.

Some view action as another form of entertainment, the specialized product of a new class of professional actors. We easily slide into the familiar and comfortable role of spectator, critic, or channel-changer.

What crystallized for me that day in Manhattan was this: what I was observing was not an action at all, but a reenactment. This reenactment—and so many others we see on television—was more theatrical than political. It was not just scripted, but plagiarized, an odd attempt literally to recreate the pain of a tribe somewhere in South America. These reenactors shared many of the qualities of those who dress up in Union or Confederate garb and reenact the greatest battles of the Civil War with obsessive attention to detail, right down to the buttons used and underwear worn by the soldiers themselves. Tony Horwitz's fine book, *Confederates in the Attic,* provides a sensitive and disturbing account of this world.

What began, perhaps, as an attempt to honor the actions of others, had lost contact with its source and had become disturbingly self-involved. Jaroslav Pelikan, the renowned religious historian, wrote, "An idol purports to be the embodiment of that which it represents, but it directs us to itself rather than beyond itself." These demonstrators were doing just that, directing the noonday crowd, the police, and the media that never appeared, to themselves, not beyond themselves. They were political idolaters.

The cops in lower Manhattan were beyond bored. They had seen this all before. They had studied the tactics of the past and fine-tuned their security, media, and public relations responses. They were smart enough, for the most part, to avoid repeating their own past overreactions. They practiced more creative, subtle, and sophisticated responses. They had learned how *not* to react—thus depriving the civil rights reenactors, environmental reenactors, or global warming reenactors of the satisfaction of a response.

Meanwhile, the great American middle—moderate and pivotal, the supposed audience of this action—has rightfully tired of this spectacle. Most Americans can't imagine themselves doused with black paint, lying on a sidewalk, amid hustling shoppers and observant cops. If this is "action," if this is public engagement, if this is what you need to do to get attention, recognition, and response, then most people will just dash past, play solitaire on the office computer, or pray that their college-aged kids grow out of this fad and apply to business school.

While it makes perfect sense to reject these reenactments, it is dangerous to reject the habit of genuine public action. It's damaging to the health of a democracy that developed out of the creative and measured actions of thousands of ordinary men and women. Americans in the late eighteenth century engaged in hundreds of actions, large and small, from local confrontations with British tax collectors to the formation of a shadow government, before they resorted, grudgingly, to the titanic action of a protracted Revolutionary War. The well-being of American workers only began to improve when workers acted to organize their plants and shops. Our freedoms have been deepened and renewed by the everyday and often unrecorded actions of citizens who demanded voting rights, civil rights, and better schools.

But constructive and creative action doesn't just happen. Rosa Parks didn't wake up one morning and spontaneously decide to sit on a seat near the front of the bus. She thought about her nonviolent but high-risk action and debated it with other leaders. She trained at the Highlander Folk School, in the mountains of Tennessee, where civil rights leaders and organizers systematically educated themselves on the strategies and tactics of others in history who had sought social change.

In effect, she studied the forgotten phonics and lost language of public action. She mastered this vocabulary, with depth and discipline, and then "spoke" to her fellow leaders and followers, to the media and to moderates, in a unique and innovative way. She demonstrated, once again, that an ordinary American could learn about action, could lead the action, and then could transmit the lessons and limitations of that action to others.

Our national vitality—the critical counterpart to our national security—depends on our willingness and ability to brush up on these lessons and skills.

CHAPTER 4

Introducing Your Larger Self

In the early stages of the development of East Brooklyn Congregations, after thousands of individual meetings and scores of training sessions, after one hundred house meetings and extensive analysis of issues and concerns, after scores of talented leaders began to emerge from these meetings, we began a series of "introductory" actions. Each action involved specific issues that needed resolution. But addressing the issues was not the primary purpose of these actions. Each action was designed to introduce our leaders to other power players in the city, to communicate that this organization was not just *another* group but a different *kind* of group, and to shatter any stereotypes that others might have about us. We were after much more than attention: we sought something different and deeper, called recognition.

Intelligent action, even public confrontation, is at bottom an attempt to engage and relate. Most activists fail to appreciate this. Bureaucrats seek to stifle it. Reenactors have lost sight of it. Celebrity self-promoters try to monopolize it. And terrorists long to destroy it. Our leaders study and practice it. Recognition is fundamental—the most basic sign of respect, the start of reciprocity, and the precondition for a working public relationship.

One early action focused on the city's director of major construction projects. In several house meetings, leaders mentioned that a very important park and pool—the Betsy Head Park and Pool—had been closed for several years for renovation. The problem was that very little renovation had taken place. We put together a research team of leaders and learned that about 80 percent of the three million dollars budgeted for the renovation had been spent but that only about 15 percent of the needed work had been completed. Armed with these facts, we called the city's construction director for a meeting.

Alice McCollum headed a team of twelve leaders the morning of the meeting. Mrs. McCollum, a bright, middle-aged African American, who was a leader in her Baptist church, was a single mother of ten children who lived directly across the street from the closed park and pool. Her younger children had all made great use of the recreation facility when it had opened. For years now, they'd had no place to play except the bleak courtyard of her apartment complex.

The game plan for the meeting was straightforward. Mrs. McCollum would thank the director for the meeting, lead our group in the rounds, explain what our research had uncovered, and then ask one simple question: "When do you expect to complete the renovation of Betsy Head Park and Pool?" We knew that the city officials would try to distract us from this fundamental matter. But that—the completion of the facility—was the specific issue that concerned us.

The director considered himself a liberal, a proud alumnus of the progressive Lindsay administration who was now serving Mayor Koch. He welcomed our group enthusiastically and said that he was pleased that so many people had taken the time to visit him in the middle of the day. "This is really democracy in action. This is something Thomas Jefferson would appreciate and applaud. This is what makes New York . . ."

Alice McCollum gently interrupted. "Sir, when do you expect to complete the renovation of Betsy Head Park and Pool?"

"Before we get into details, let me introduce my assistant and the fine staff of this department. These are the people who make the city run as well as it does. First, on my left, is Mr. . . ."

"I'm sorry to interrupt again," said Mrs. McCollum, even more moderately, "but when do you expect to complete the renovation of Betsy Head Park and Pool?"

"Well," said the director, "we have done some research into this matter. It is very very complicated, with many contractual considerations that would just bore you all this morning."

"Sir," said Mrs. McCollum, her voice lower and softer. The room was very quiet now. The director was standing at the head of the boardroom table, with three staff people seated around him. Our team of twelve was arrayed around the table. Mrs. McCollum was seated at the far end, directly opposite the director. "When do you expect to complete the renovation of Betsy Head Park and Pool?"

The director's positive and upbeat tone had disappeared. He seemed, suddenly, sullen. "I don't know what you think gives you the right to come in here and raise your voice and treat me this way. You think this is the only project behind schedule?"

Alice McCollum raised her hand very slowly, like a teacher calming a student, and whispered, "When do you expect to complete the renovation of Betsy Head . . . ?"

The director exploded, "You people! You people! How dare you?" Now, everyone in East Brooklyn, everyone black or Hispanic, everyone who has watched taxis rush past them on a street at night or stood in line in a welfare office knows what the phrase "you people" means when it's used by a white person in power. It means, "You nobodies. You uppity minorities. You interlopers." And worse.

Alice McCollum went for the jugular in a voice so soft that you would only have known what she was saying because you had heard her repeat it four previous times, "When do you expect to complete the renovation of Betsy Head Park and Pool?"

The director was screaming now. Thomas Jefferson, the sage of Monticello, the theorist of democracy in action, the Lindsay years, the New York melting pot—these were all distant memories. Mrs. McCollum shut her notebook, put her pen in her handbag, and stood. The closing of the notebook was our cue: we all collected our materials and stood as well. Silently, she led us out of the room and down the hallway. The director followed us to the door and yelled down the hallway as we waited for the elevator. When we all got in the elevator and the door finally closed, the entire group exhaled. We could hear him screaming, high above us, his screams growing fainter and fainter, as the elevator descended.

In the evaluation in the lobby downstairs, I asked the leaders how they felt. "Whew," one leader said. "Shocked," some said. "Surprised," others said. "I've never seen anything like that," one said. I turned to Alice McCollum and asked her how she felt. She thought for several seconds. "I have never felt so much in control in any meeting ever. *We* were in control. And I feel we are going to win."

We had planned this action carefully and role-played it repeatedly. I had warned the leaders that if the director overreacted we should watch out for two tendencies—the tendency to argue back and the tendency to giggle out of nervousness. No one said a word in the meeting. No one laughed or smiled or nodded his or her head to break the ice. The discipline, as the director unraveled and became more and more volatile, was superb. The group followed

Alice McCollum's excellent leadership as if it had been training for this event for years. We had gotten more of a reaction than we had bargained for by being simple and quiet and focused—not by waving a sign or shouting a slogan. And we knew that, because the director did consider himself a Lindsay-era progressive, he would be worried about who we would speak to about his overreaction. The media? The mayor? Other political leaders in the city? We decided to do nothing right away. We agreed to just let him react for a few days to his own overreaction.

Several days later, work crews appeared at Betsy Head Park and Pool. The renovation went on at a feverish pace after years of delay. Within months, the entire facility was upgraded, and the city scheduled a grand reopening. Our team attended. On the dais, sat the director, with other city officials. Alice McCollum approached him. He nearly flinched as she walked up to him. She smiled a broad, warm, welcoming smile and stuck out her hand. "Congratulations," she said. "We appreciate your prompt response and your fine work. You've returned to our children a place to swim and play." The director was wary. Slowly, he extended his hand and thanked Mrs. McCollum. From that day on, he was one of the most responsive and professional public officials that our leaders had the pleasure to relate to.

Whatever stereotype the director and his staff may have had of leaders from East Brooklyn—easily put off, not well informed, thrilled to be complimented by a powerful city official, or, even more negatively, ragtag, loud, unorganized, gullible—was shattered by the precision of the action Alice McCollum led. He recognized her, the quality of her organization, and her ability to turn the tables on him. And whatever preconceptions our leaders may have had about a high-level government official—professional, knowledgeable, in charge, unflappable—evaporated as well. They learned how to agitate a public official. They learned how quiet discipline often is more effective than loud and chaotic activity.

They learned how to stifle their own nervousness and follow a capable and powerful local leader. And they learned, at the groundbreaking, months later, the value of depolarizing a situation once a public official has responded effectively.

Several months later, still focused on the issue of recognition, we had scheduled two meetings, back to back, with the city's housing and sanitation commissioners. The adviser to the mayor coordinating the two meetings reserved a beautiful City Hall hearing room, called the Blue Room, for the sessions. The day before the meetings, Stephen Roberson, the EBC associate organizer, went down to City Hall to scout out the space. When he returned for the final briefing meeting that night, he sketched on the chalkboard the layout of the room. At the head of the room was a raised dais, with fifteen very plush leather chairs. In front of each chair was a microphone. Here, on high, in comfort, powerful public officials were supposed to sit. In the center of the room, in a cluster, were eight or so rickety wooden chairs—places for the peons. We stared at Stephen's drawing and started to discuss the possibility of arriving a little early and occupying the fifteen leather chairs.

The next day we arrived twenty minutes early for our two o'clock meeting. No one greeted us at the door of City Hall. No one escorted us to the Blue Room. So we found our way there and entered. The room was empty. The fifteen chairs beckoned. Reverend Youngblood was the key spokesperson for our team, so he sat in the central chair, with seven other EBC leaders and staff arrayed on either side of him. We occupied every chair and the entire dais.

At two o'clock sharp, the city's housing commissioner, Anthony Gliedman, a large man, balding at an early age, who was energetic and savvy, entered the room with an entourage of four aides. He moved toward the dais, saw us arranged there, and joked, "Hey, what's the matter here? Are we under indictment or something?"

"Not yet," said Reverend Youngblood, also joking.

Commissioner Gliedman took a few more steps toward the dais. "Ummm, we'd like to join you up there . . ."

Reverend Youngblood looked up and down the table. The chairs were occupied by an EBC leader, several elderly women, two elderly men, two other pastors, Stephen Roberson, and me. "Well, we're already settled in up here, and we know that you wouldn't want any of the senior citizens who have come today to move."

"Uh, no," said Gliedman, clearly seeing the problem he faced, "but how about if we bring these wooden chairs up there . . ."

"I don't think that would work," said Reverend Youngblood, "We wouldn't be able to see you over this high dais. So why don't you just sit right there, where we usually do?"

Gliedman hesitated, and then slowly, reluctantly, lowered himself onto one of the wooden chairs. It creaked a bit. His staff followed his lead. I have never seen five more uncomfortable men. They weren't just physically uncomfortable, they were *politically* uncomfortable. They were having the tables turned on them, literally, and they couldn't figure out how to respond.

Reverend Youngblood led them through our agenda of housing issues that we had set up for the day. Then, at the end, after fifteen minutes, he told the commissioner how much we appreciated his time and said, "Thank you for coming."

"Thank you . . ." Gliedman muttered, mostly to himself.

We remained in our chairs as Gliedman and his crew stormed out of the room. We knew that, out in the hallway, the second commissioner and his staff were mustering. We would no longer have the benefit of surprise. We could hear the two teams of city officials arguing in loud voices—the housing team exasperated and outraged by being told to sit in the citizens' section and the sanitation team declaring that they would never submit to such a humiliation.

The doors banged open and the sanitation commissioner led a

kind of charge. He and the three aides with him marched right past the wooden chairs and right up to the dais. We looked down on four red, frustrated faces—their chins at the level of the dais.

"Anything wrong?" Reverend Youngblood asked, clearly enjoying the dynamic, as was the rest of our team.

The sanitation commissioner realized that he could not lead his men over the top of the dais. He had only two choices, retreat back to the wooden chairs or just leave the room entirely. He opted for the chairs. Fifteen minutes later, we thanked them for coming and ended the second meeting.

Just when we thought the day couldn't get any better, it did. Both commissioners, in high dudgeon, went over to the City Hall press room, Room 9, and complained about how we had treated them, how our leaders had occupied all of the best chairs, how they had been made to sit in the wooden seats, and how they had been thanked for coming by upstarts from some godforsaken corner of Brooklyn. The reporters, intrigued by this tale of woe, rushed over to the Blue Room and interviewed our leaders. Several filed stories about this new group, from the boondocks of East Brooklyn, that had had the temerity to turn the tables on two city commissioners.

Six months later, after a follow-up meeting with the housing commissioner, Tony Gliedman said that he wanted to ask us a question that had been really bothering him. "That day in the Blue Room—what was that really about?"

"Recognition," I said.

Gliedman sat quietly and thought. "Now I get it," he said. And, more importantly, he had begun to get *us*.

But his boss, the mayor, Edward I. Koch, feisty and aggressive in this phase between the end of his first term and the start of his second, had not. We were just beginning to get to know Ed Koch at the time, not through direct contact (this was years before my memorable evening at Gracie Mansion), because that was quite limited, but more through our dealings with his aides, deputies, and commissioners, and through the sources we had begun to develop in the press. The Ed Koch who emerged through this period was—and still is—a complex man. He had the ability to attract and retain some of the finest women and men we have encountered in public life. Gordon Davis, Stan Brezenoff, Felice Michetti, Lilliam Barrios Paoli, Herman Badillo, Jeremy Travis, and the late Bobby Wagner—it would be hard to imagine a more diverse, more talented, and often more contentious group.

Koch had other qualities that we grew to admire. He had the capacity to work with those he distrusted or disliked—people like us. He could rally the city and represent the city at crucial times. And he wasn't pretty or slick: he had the face and physique of a normal person.

In late 1981 and early 1982, as we began to negotiate with the city the terms of what became known as the East Brooklyn Congregations Nehemiah Plan, we noticed that he would not say the name of the organization. He would not utter "East Brooklyn Congregations," "EBC," or "Industrial Areas Foundation." Instead, he referred to us as "those churches," "the religious people," or some other half-descriptive, half-dismissive term. He would always act exceedingly gracious in the presence of our strongest ally, Bishop Mugavero, whom he adored and who eventually received the prestigious La Guardia Medal from the mayor, but would be cooler, harsher, and more hostile to the rest of us. Privately, he referred to us, as he did to many he disagreed with, as "wackos."

As we prepared to begin construction on our first one thousand homes, we invited the mayor to attend the ground-breaking ceremony. After all, the city had agreed, after much tugging and pulling, to provide the land and the subsidy to allow us to build our homes. We told the mayor that we would turn out five thousand

EBC members for the outdoor event. We had hired a bulldozer to break the ground, not just a few shovels. And we expected plenty of press.

We then asked the mayor if he would be willing to lead the countdown for the ground-breaking—the ten, nine, eight that would lead to the moment the bulldozer bit into the earth. The mayor expressed surprise. Our invitation for him to play the central role, the master of ceremonies, at the pivotal moment, with the crowd cheering and the cameras flashing, caught him off guard. Really? He asked. Yes, we said. He accepted.

When he arrived on Stone Avenue (now Mother Gaston Boulevard) on the afternoon of the ground-breaking, he was excited. Reverend Youngblood, Reverend John Heinemeier, Fr. John Powis, Alice McCollum, Celina Jamieson, and I greeted him and said that we would like to prepare him for the countdown. We sat in a circle on the stage, with the enormous crowd building before us and the bulldozer growling in the rubble, and informed the mayor how the countdown should go: "ten-EBC, nine-EBC, eight-EBC, seven-EBC . . ." He looked up at me and barked, "You son of a . . ." "six-EBC, five-EBC."

We weren't sure what the mayor would say or do until he went to the podium, nodded to the bulldozer, and began the countdown. He dutifully said "EBC" ten straight times. The bulldozer surged forward and scooped an enormous load of brick, broken glass, and dirt out of the field of rubble. The crowd roared—fifty-five hundred midwives—at the sounds and sights of the community being reborn.

In the photos we've kept from that day, the mayor doesn't appear particularly pleased. We, on the other hand, are grinning like crazy. From that afternoon on, the mayor used our name, not some weak substitute, whenever he referred to us. We never failed to give

him the credit he deserved: he was willing to provide land and subsidy so that thousands of citizens could afford to buy homes of
their own. He assigned several of his most competent and creative
associates and commissioners to work with our team. And he remained in an uneasy but productive relationship with leaders he
grudgingly recognized, but clearly never "got." In the world of
power, in the world as it is, that's a pretty good deal.

CHAPTER 5

Merit Means (Almost) Nothing

Insisting on recognition, developing the power to reward and punish, practicing both flexibility and persistence—our mothers, fathers, and civics instructors rarely if ever emphasized these important public qualities.

We were taught that merit mattered. If we just presented the facts in a full and fair manner, if we got the words right, the slogan right, the tone right, the photo-op right, then others would realize the errors of their ways and move in our direction. We learned a great deal about what ought to be—how to describe it, communicate it, promote it, and defend it—and very little about the dangerous undertows and cross currents of individual and institutional interests.

We headed to the library and pored over texts. We mastered the most meritorious research work conducted by the best experts in the field. We scribbled their insights on our index cards and made our cases in long term papers and intense debates. We sat for hours in meaningless hearings so that we could fill two minutes with our distilled facts. But we spent little or no time tracing the source and the flow of money, the quirks of personality, the dense webs of relationships, or the presence and impact of evil. When our opponents remained unconvinced, when behavior did not change, when the neutral moderates failed to fill the seats and pews, we often assumed that we had failed to make a persuasive case. So some just studied harder, jotted more notes, and wrote better briefs. Others grew tired and cynical, others more isolated and self-righteous. Many activists adjusted their expectations to a lifetime of speaking out, bearing witness, and raising consciousness rather than generating reactions and making change. Moderates, sensing confusion and defeat, lost patience and did the sensible thing: got a second job or took a course, improved the yard, or finished the basement.

We constantly run across situations in our organizing where merit doesn't matter and where a different kind of response is called for. Here are just a few examples.

A number of years ago, EBC leaders who attended a series of house meetings reported that conditions in local food stores had reached a crisis level. The area was impoverished. Major chains did not serve the community. And local corner stores and midsized markets offered customers few options. Shoppers found aging meat, poor produce, coolers and freezers that barely cooled and rarely froze, dirt and dust on the shelves, and prices significantly higher than in areas and stores several miles away. The owners and managers of these stores often sat in balcony roosts, overlooking the aisles of the store, so that they could yell at anyone they suspected of shoplifting.

In a world of merit, customers would call the city or state inspection or consumer affairs departments and demand attention to these conditions. We researched both departments, met with their representatives, and learned that they were woefully understaffed and basically toothless. It would take more than a year for the state to send out an inspector and then a lot more time for the results of the inspection to be analyzed. A negative report would lead to a small fine. Many of our leaders believed that the local inspectors, when they did appear, were easily deterred by gifts of cigarettes from the store owners.

Our team decided to design its own inspection system. We pored over various inspection forms and drafted our own. We ordered buttons that said: "Official EBC Food Store Inspector." We bought clipboards and thermometers and weights and measures. We studied the rules regulating food stores and became expert at them. We role-played how a team of ten "inspectors" would enter a store and conduct a thorough review without interfering with other shoppers. And we called the police and briefed them about our plans.

On a bright Saturday, in the middle of a busy morning, one hundred inspectors, organized in teams of ten, appeared at ten different stores. Each team entered its store and began to inspect. Several people went up and down the aisles with a cart and a budget of fifty dollars. They bought the greenest meat, the fuzziest grapes, the most rusted cans, and the hardest loaves of bread they could find—which was not difficult to do in these stores. Another team went to the coolers and freezers and monitored and recorded the temperatures there. A third team did a price comparison of twenty preselected items. The impact was immediate. Other shoppers recognized the EBC "inspectors," encouraged them in their work, and brought over more evidence of shoddy merchandise and unsanitary conditions. Suddenly, the morning of shopping turned into a morning of inspecting. The stores buzzed, in a way they never had before, with complaints, information, and mutual support.

The store managers, aloft in their perches, watching the mutiny grow below, behaved in predictable ways. Some yelled—to no effect. People couldn't hear them. A few waded into the aisles and threatened our leaders with arrest. Our team leaders pointed out-side—to the police car that we had summoned to protect us from owners who might overreact. One manager tried to stop our des-ignated shoppers from purchasing the spoiled and rotten food. "Why do you want that stuff?" he pleaded. "I'll get you some good food."

We had entered the stores with EBC Letters of Agreement. Once we completed each inspection, we gave the owner a list of the conditions that required correction and asked him to sign an agreement to do so. If he refused to sign, we assured him that we would publicize in every congregation and housing project in East Brooklyn the fact that he was unwilling to maintain minimal stan-dards of cleanliness and sanitation in his store. We told him that we would be back, with larger teams of inspectors, next Saturday, every Saturday, with the media, for as long as it took for him to see the light. Seven of the owners signed that morning—eagerly, en-thusiastically, willing to do anything to get our teams out of their stores.

Three held out. The EBC leaders launched an intensive cam-paign of spot inspections for several weeks, then invited the three holdouts to a meeting of four hundred EBC members. When the three arrived to the session, in the basement of St. Paul Commu-nity Baptist Church, they were asked to wait in a quiet room out-side the assembly hall. At the designated moment, they were called in and ushered up the center aisle, right in front of the podium oc-cupied by a young and forceful Roman Catholic priest, Fr. Leo Penta. Fr. Penta read them the riot act and told them that the days of bullying, abuse, and dehumanizing conditions in the food stores of East Brooklyn were over. Then, in a powerful voice, filled with authority, he intoned, "You are dismissed." For a moment, the hall was still, stunned. These petty autocrats, these men who humili-ated shoppers as they searched filthy aisles for better prices and decent food, turned on their heels and hurried out of the room. Then the audience exploded—with humor, with joy, and with a new appreciation of their own potential and power. The three signed within days—but not before one tried to bribe a leader with a case of cigarettes.

The one hundred leaders who spearheaded this action celebrated their victory and began to digest the important lessons learned. If the formal process doesn't work, or, worse yet, is a fraud and a trap, don't waste much time depending on it. Figure out how to create your own. If the existing authority has collapsed, if the inspectors and the agencies and the local politicians have abdicated, then carefully and playfully generate your own authoritative approach. If the owners won't respond for the right reasons, because it is wrong to cheat and overcharge and verbally abuse responsible shoppers, than make it clear that they might consider responding for other reasons. They may not want ongoing inspections. They may lose business to the stores that do comply. They may cringe when they read about themselves in the *Daily News.* And leave race, class, and faith out of it. It was easy in this case, because the ten owners were wonderfully diverse. But even if they are not, stay focused on the basic conditions. Don't whine. Don't dwell on discontent. Don't rely on the merits. Take charge. Be irreverent. Test how plastic the world really is. And learn how to enjoy a win.

Two more stories from Chicago illustrate this point. In the late seventies, a developer on the northwest side proposed to build a condominium complex in a quiet neighborhood of single-family homes. The local homeowners, many of whom were leaders in our organization there, objected. The condominium complex would tower over the bungalows and alter the nature of the community. The research we did was not encouraging, though. The developer had bought the property. The zoning permitted the use he hoped to construct there. And the local Democratic Party leaders were in the developer's pocket. There would be hearings, meetings, protests, and the like, but the fix, literally, was already in.

One afternoon, a team of leaders examined the property and took a closer look at an old and long-abandoned farmhouse there. It was a terribly sorry sight—unpainted, sagging, tilting to one side. On a hunch, we decided to do a title search of the house. We discovered that a farmer named Rinker had built the home in the 1800s. It was no longer a decrepit and potentially dangerous structure. It had historical value. We called in the preservationists, who found an intricate and rare form of woodworking done by the craftsmen who designed the windows and the eaves of the home. The home had architectural and aesthetic qualities that were rare.

Our leaders shifted away from the issues of the height, density, and neighborhood impact of the condominium—the merits of the case—and repeated a theme that they couldn't have cared less about: "Save the Rinker House!" The media echoed the cry. And suddenly the developer and his political supporters found themselves on the defensive.

The developer became desperate as the tide of publicity turned. After all, he had bought the property. He had made all of the obligatory contributions to local politicians and party faithful. He had played by the both the written and unwritten rules of the city at the time—and was stuck with a piece of land that had lost most of its value because of the presence of a shack. He thought he had a solution to his problems.

Our leaders woke up one morning and looked out their back windows. The Rinker House had disappeared. In the middle of the night, a truck had pulled up, hauling a bulldozer. The bulldozer had made quick and quiet work of the house, smashing the rare filigree to smithereens with the rest of the structure, before being towed away. We cried foul, and the press had a field day. It didn't take long for the police to identify the owner of the bulldozer, to track the bulldozer owner to the developer, and to assemble sufficient evidence to indict him for his desperate act of demolition. Months later, the threat of towering condominiums receded as the powerful developer caught in a relatively petty offense trudged off to jail. Another, more famous, Chicagoan, Al Capone, went to prison for *tax evasion,* the least of his crimes, not for murder, fraud, assault, burglary, bribing city officials, corrupting cops, or bootlegging.

Around the same time, back at Our Lady of the Angels, a team of leaders struggled with a sensitive and dangerous development. A group of drug dealers had set up shop on the street corner right outside the office of the school's principal—Sr. Marian Murphy. Every day, through the afternoon, even at dismissal time, the dealers dominated the corner and sold drugs to cars that seemed to line up as soon as the sellers arrived and to older kids in the school. Sr. Marion could see and hear it all, could reach out and touch some of the sellers from her window.

The same school that had burned in 1958, the same neighborhood that had smoldered and resegregated in the late 1960s, was now seared by open, flagrant, constant drug dealing. Sr. Marion did what citizens are supposed to do. She called the local precinct, the Shakespeare District, and reported the crime. No response. Then she called again. Still no response. Then she kept a log of all of the times and days that she called and what the response was—a neat notebook filled with dates, times, and precise descriptions. She was direct, low-key, and unrelenting. She earned an A+ in surveillance. She had called the cops more than forty times. The police, for the most part, did not respond, and, when they did, they drove by belatedly, long after the dealers had dispersed.

Sr. Marion, on her own, began to film the drug dealers from her office. They had become so emboldened, they saw no reason to hide their faces or secrete their drugs, so she recorded everything on tape. Because we knew that the police couldn't be called in, and we had no idea how the police commissioner would respond, we took Sr. Marion's tape and the entire story to the local CBS affiliate. Bill Kurtis was the affiliate's young, up-and-coming anchor at the time. He liked what he saw and was particularly impressed by the principal's courage and spunk. So he assigned a camera crew to film the drug dealing as well.

It was December in Chicago—a bitter December, with deep snow and layers of ice on the sidewalks and the streets. One afternoon, as I left the rectory after a planning meeting, I noticed a police cruiser parked right behind my Dodge. I inched very slowly from the curb, west on Iowa Street. The cop fell right in behind me. On the slick street, I could go no faster than fifteen miles per hour. After a block or so, the cop flashed his lights and pulled me over.

The only thought I had was to jump out of the car, get to the middle of the street, and be *seen* by somebody. But the streets were deserted. The two-flats looked dark in the dull dusk. Sensible people huddled inside. The cop climbed out of his car and walked right up to me. He was young, in his twenties, tall, blond, severe. He moved closer to me, right in my face.

"You're going too fast," he said.

"What?"

"You're going way too fast. And if you keep it up, you're going to get hurt."

Then he moved away and returned to his car. I stood in the street until the cruiser had gone. Then I went home and discussed with my wife whether or not this was the time to leave town for a while.

Sr. Marion and our team of leaders had nowhere to go. So we urged CBS to get out there quickly. The word was out. The cops knew. Which meant the drug dealers might know as well. The camera crew arrived on a Monday—in the middle of a blizzard. No dealing that day. The second day was the same—nothing but blowing snow and a quiet street corner. The reporter and camera crew grew impatient, grumbled about all of the traffic accidents they could be covering, and began to doubt us.

On the third day, they called to say that they couldn't make it. We were both frustrated and afraid. We thought about it for a while and decided to call the CBS people back and thank them for their interest. We were sure that they wouldn't mind if we took the story to another channel.

An hour later, they were on the third floor of the school, with their camera in place and a microphone, dangled by a wire, slipped down a crease in the side of the building, so that it could pick up the sounds of the drug dealing at street level. The weather was better. The dealers returned. The corner became a lively marketplace. The CBS crew shot all the footage it needed.

On the night the story appeared—the lead story, an exclusive, with graphic shots of the dealers and the buyers—all hell broke loose. Cops seemed to be everywhere. Dealers trooped into paddy wagons all over the area. Little did we know that the media-savvy precinct commander had tipped off the ABC affiliate and had given it an exclusive: Police Respond. Dealing Derailed. Commander Cripples Crime. Saves the "Angels" of OLA.

We used the sudden notoriety to push forward on a wide variety of fronts—demanding meetings with city officials on sanitation, housing, and other issues that had been stalled for months. Commissioners who had refused to meet could not do enough for the children and families of Our Lady of the Angels. Would they meet with us? Of course. Did we need to come downtown? No. They would come to us, with cameras in tow, to solve whatever problems we presented. Even Phil Donahue called, inviting Sr. Marion to appear on his show.

For a week or so, public officials rushed to do the right thing for the wrong reason. We played it out as far as it would go. Then the media drifted away. The commissioners returned to their downtown lairs. The precinct commander was promoted, not investigated or dismissed. And we took a break—tired out by the tension of the days leading up to the CBS story and the energy it took to take advantage of the opportunities that developed during our week or so in the media sun.

In these cases, we had become experts in freezer temperature standards, farmhouse architecture, drug selling patterns, police response, regulatory authority and effectiveness, but we knew that the facts and the merits, the research and the tactics, in and of themselves, did not matter. Even worse, focusing on these issues diverted attention away from what was most important. The leaders themselves—their grit and their spirit, their discipline and playfulness, their willingness to imagine and take risk—mattered more than anything. They mastered the facts and understood the merits as a small part of their preparation for new and creative public action. But they themselves, in the planning, execution, and evaluation of these actions, were the heart and soul of this new machine.

CHAPTER 6

Chutzpah Helps

This may be all well and good for leaders of organizations trying to deal with mayors, governors, and local elected officials, with school boards, state authorities, and lending institutions, with drug problems, housing problems, and municipal wage standards, but what about the "bigger" picture—the nation? The question is valid and important, and I will spend the next section describing how we have begun to answer it. But, first, a few cautions.

Those who want to make an impact on the nation often have contempt for the local. They have grand ideas and interesting notions but no appetite for building relationships, no patience for the daily deal-making that goes on within institutions and between institutions, and no respect for the art of politics and inevitability of compromise. One frustrated foundation executive told an IAF team one day, "Most groups come in here with a Washington address and a national website and a claim to influence this policy and that policy—and have no local base, no strength, no leverage. You are just the opposite. You have a local base, plenty of strength, lots of leverage—and no national presence or impact."

We argued with her. We don't see the value in practicing politics deductively—taking a position, marshalling our arguments, making our case, finding a celebrity or media champion, and mixing with other experts and upper-middle managers in conferences in the Capitol. Thousand of worthy and not so worthy groups already operate this way. It's as if everyone wants to be a futures trader on the commodities market, and no one wants to plow the soil, plant the seeds, tend the crop, and harvest the fields. We want to do both. But we know that we need to work inductively, through the process of individual meetings and house meetings, through the acquired habits of action and evaluation, and through the testing and retesting of ideas and strategies in cities and states, before we bring these matters to a broader market and before our leaders can effectively play a broader role.

During the 2000 presidential election campaign, the leaders of the IAF organizations in the Northeast, especially from Boston to Washington, organized a series of actions designed to begin to inject the lessons of our larger local successes into the national debate. More importantly, the actions were an opportunity to showcase a growing group of leaders who had succeeded for years in their cities and states but who needed new arenas, new stages, new audiences, and new opponents to engage.

I wish that I could say that this decision to engage the two lead presidential candidates was rooted in the purest of motives and most careful considerations of strategy. We were confident of our motives. And we thought through various strategies. But impatience, frustration, and anger all played prominent roles, as well. After all, we had suffered through eight years of Ronald Reagan, four years of George Herbert Walker Bush, and another eight years of William Jefferson Clinton—twenty years, three presidents, two parties, various congressional configurations, and little more than occasional sops cast in the direction of the cities.

We lived and worked in those cities—particularly in the Northeast and Midwest—places that continued to burn, shrink, and decline. Or we sat in traffic in the surrounding suburbs, which sprawled further and further into the countryside. We watched president after president offer slogans and sideshows—points of light, volunteerism crusades, new markets initiatives, empowerment zones, so-called faith-based solutions—to the families and individuals caught in a dynamic that went far beyond the block busting and panic peddling of the sixties.

This was neighborhood busting, city busting, and region busting—on a scale and at a cost that could not have been imagined thirty years before. New hustlers peddling sub-prime loans replaced the contract sellers of the sixties. The currency exchanges became currency consumers—extracting higher and higher fees for every financial transaction and creating new forms of usury called payday loans. Townshiplike conditions that used to occur only in central cities and in the rural South began to appear on Long Island and in Maryland and Georgia suburbs.

This was one reality. The second reality was the durability, resilience, and faithfulness of a group of people we began to call the critical mass class. They were the vast majority of hardworking families who didn't need much from society. They didn't need an alphabet soup of liberal programs spooned out by the social workers of the left or a series of fundamentalist sermons delivered by conservative prophets about the magic of the market. They needed what most Americans have always needed: a job that paid a living wage, an opportunity to build equity through the purchase of a home that they could afford or a business they could buy, and an institution or set of institutions that would defend and promote their values and interests—a congregation, a party, or an organization. Put these three basics together, and the members of the critical mass class would create their own chain reaction. They would sustain their families and raise their kids, invest their savings and improve their homes, participate in their local schools and hold political figures accountable, lead, argue, cooperate, contend, be fuller members of society, be better and sharper citizens. Day in and day out, year in and year out, we moved among an army of fit and loyal Americans—rarely called to serve, often injured by the society they still pledged their allegiance to.

Then there was a third reality. We did not need government to come up with creative solutions to the challenges of the critical mass class. The leaders of that class—working through our organizations and others—already had. Or had in part. In Baltimore, beginning in 1994, our local IAF organization launched the nation's first living wage campaign. The effort focused on the wages paid by bus companies, janitorial firms, and security companies hired by the city. These companies often paid their workers minimum wages with no benefits and often no guarantee of a fixed number of hours employment. Parents couldn't plan child care and day care, didn't know how much they would work or make, couldn't afford a telephone, electricity, or an apartment or home of their own. Our leaders and these workers saw no reason for the city to be saving money in the short term by underpaying workers, who then had to use an exhausting variety of government and charitable programs to supplement the lack of a living wage. The BUILD organization successfully designed and passed a bill raising workers wages incrementally from $4.25 to $8.80 an hour, over three years—enough to begin to allow workers to approximate a decent life and not enough to break the city's bank. In 1996, the organizations in New York passed the second living wage bill. Since then, more than forty local living wage bills had been passed. Now the IAF groups in the Northeast were asking the two presidential candidates to consider a living wage standard for all companies that benefited in any way from government contracts or subsidies—everyone from defense contractors to religious home health care groups, from major banks to local community development corporations.

The other solution authored by the IAF was visible on the streets of East Brooklyn and the South Bronx, Baltimore and West Philadelphia. More than four thousand new Nehemiah homes—single family, owner occupied, and affordable—stood on blocks that had burned, crumbled, and nearly disappeared. Children played in the new backyards. Neighbors sat on stoops. One single woman, no taller than five feet, in her fifties, a native of Trinidad, talked about taking a walk—a walk!—for an hour each night through the streets of East New York. The soft slap of her shoes on the new sidewalks of those rebuilt blocks was the sound of victory.

So, we weren't approaching the candidates with intractable problems. We were interested in presenting to them solutions that we had devised in our local political "skunk works"—our local laboratories of public participation and social problem solving. We knew that we could create significant impact in the cities and counties where we had working organizations—sixty or so large communities around the country. But there were hundreds more where the same issues existed. And a national emphasis on practical solutions to immediate problems would accelerate the pace of change for the reliable members of the critical mass class.

Instead of an agreement to meet with a top team of our leaders, we heard from both camps how the candidates had been converted to "faith-based solutions" and "faith-based initiatives." By this, they did not mean modest increases in wages or a national campaign to build homes that those earning twenty-five thousand dollars a year could afford. No, they focused on the role that religious organizations play in providing social services. And they competed with one another in their zeal to convince the electorate how poorly government performed these tasks. We had no argument with the often-impressive impact created by religious groups in the delivery of social services. There was nothing new or different about this. What we did object to was the implication that chronic national problems could somehow be solved by the good works of a few churches. And we grew suspicious of candidates who soaked their speeches in religious rhetoric and who seemed to substitute personal piety for public works.

We rejected the tag—faith based—that the candidates wished to impose on us, just as we resisted the alternatives used by Mayor Koch. And we wanted to have an opportunity to speak directly with then Governor Bush and then Vice President Gore about these important matters of city-building, of nation-building, and of the appropriate use of public sector power.

You might think that candidates interested in the work of faith-based groups would be eager to meet with one of the largest and most effective organizers of local religious institutions in the nation. That was not our experience.

We wrote, called, and spoke with many aides. But the candidates would not meet. Junior aides would meet. Policy advisers would meet. One very senior aide could not believe that we would not accept him as a substitute for the candidate. "You must not know how important I am," he said, to Sr. Kathy Maire. "The fact that I'm willing to meet is unprecedented." Unprecedented or not, we refused. And we set off to try to engage the candidates directly.

Our first attempt was on a January day in Wilmington. The Delaware Republican Party announced a luncheon for the presidential candidate at the Hotel DuPont. Tickets were available, so we reserved two tables, eighteen seats, for the pleasure of hearing George W. Bush and perhaps being able to ask a question in the brief period that would follow his remarks.

Early that morning, 12 January, a fax arrived at our Philadelphia office from the Delaware Republicans. That fax stated that they had oversold the luncheon and that that table reserved in my name had been canceled. They apologized for the inconvenience. Clearly, they had been reading the papers and listening to the radio. On the day before, our leaders had held a press conference right across the street from the White House, in the Episcopal Church of St. John's at Lafayette Square, to urge the candidates to drop the superficial religiosity and to address more practically issues of concern to scores of millions of Americans. The press event was cochaired by Reverend Youngblood and Arnie Graf of the IAF and included religious leaders from all across the political spectrum—Bishop John Hurst Adams of the African Methodist Episcopal Church, Bishop David Benke of the Missouri Synod Lutheran Church, Rabbi Saperstein of the Association of Reformed Rabbis, Episcopal Bishop Ronald Haines, and a top assistant to Cardinal Hickey. Religious leaders called on the candidates to use less religious rhetoric—a story that many news services picked up on. The Delaware Republicans were listening, saw my name and IAF's name on the reservation, and canceled our table. They failed to notice a second table reserved by a registered Republican who was also a part of our nonpartisan network, Catherine Poneros. We decided to claim those nine reserved seats, if possible.

Our team met in the lobby of the old, elegant Hotel DuPont at half past ten. The "we" that day was eighteen leaders—nine whites and nine blacks, four organizers and fourteen leaders. Audrey Russell was there—an African American woman, a senior citizen with sore and painful legs, an active Lutheran leader from northwest Philadelphia. So was Rabbi Ivan Caine, moderate and professorial, even-tempered and judicious, the leader of Society Hill Synagogue in Philadelphia. Ben Contee had taken the early train from Washington. Mr. Contee, a retired city worker, was quiet, serious, steady, a cochairman of our Washington organization. He had traveled up to Delaware with Martin Trimble, the energetic lead organizer of the Washington group, the son of the former rector of the venerable Christ Episcopal Church in Philadelphia, where George Washington worshiped and Benjamin Franklin is buried. Marvin Calloway was assisting me today. Marvin, like Martin, is about forty, the father of three, a product of a single mother and a tough housing project in the South Bronx. He worked as a carpenter before beginning a career in organizing.

Our leaders may have been a little older, a little grayer, perhaps even a little more moderate than other IAF teams, but not by much. They didn't think of themselves as activists. They wouldn't feel comfortable among those who blew whistles and broke windows at the World Trade Organization meeting in Seattle. Or among the ardent followers of Charlton Heston, another virtual Hollywood hero, and his confreres at the NRA. They were deep, experienced, thoughtful people—citizens of a nation, not activists in a cause. They were confident of one another, in the lessons they had learned in their local work, and in the organizing staff that supported them. They were nervous about what might happen that day, sure that they belonged there, and game for whatever may come.

Our plan was straightforward: to pick up the remaining seats we had reserved and attend the luncheon; to listen respectfully to the candidate and to try to pose a question in the period after his remarks; and to approach the most senior aide on the scene after the event and pursue the scheduling of a meeting with the candidate himself. We also planned to speak with as many of the scores of reporters present as possible about the themes and issues we had outlined the day before in Washington. We were armed with a simple, four-page description of our approach and a one-page summary of the living wage and Nehemiah strategies we had pioneered.

Most of the other four hundred or so people gathering for the luncheon were wealthy and white. They mingled easily in the lobby as they waited to pay for their seats and enter the dining room. We approached the tables where well-dressed women were taking people's checks and assigning seats. On the tables, we saw our name tags—neatly filled out, waiting for us to claim them. But when Catherine Poneros introduced herself to the greeter and began to write a check, she was told that her table was no longer available as well.

Eighteen of us were now standing in a small cluster, surrounded by scores of others easily securing their seats and heading in, asking about our reservations. The courteous women behind the tables did not know what to say. So they called the hotel manager over. He was a short, round, affable fellow, who couldn't figure out what had gone wrong but did know that we couldn't go in. We objected and asked to speak to a Bush staff person.

Another man—younger, fresh-faced, crisp—appeared. We summarized our situation. The young man said he too was sorry, as sorry as the luncheon manager, but there was nothing that he could do. At this point, one of our team, an Episcopal clergywoman, who was participating in her first action, said to me that she couldn't believe that this was happening to us, to her, in her home city, in America. Another clergyman, a local AME pastor, with a long and distinguished history of service in the city, expressed to the rest of our team how embarrassed—flabbergasted— he was by the treatment we were receiving.

The young Bush aide left, and a security person materialized. We now noticed that a line of about ten security personnel had set itself up between our group and the door of the hotel dining room. They had been watching too many television shows. They had established a defensive perimeter against moderate citizens—Audrey Russell and her arthritic knees, Rabbi Caine and his patrician manner, Ben Contee and his working-class respectfulness and formality—who had been denied seats that they had responsibly reserved well ahead of time. Couldn't they look at the faces of our leaders and realize that rushing into the luncheon was the absolute last thing that these leaders would ever do?

The stern security man insisted we leave the lobby immediately. We asked why. He said the fire marshals had told him that we posed a danger if we remained congregated near the door. We asked him to point the fire marshal out, but the security man refused. He kept intoning, "You must now leave the foyer," as if addressing a crowd of hundreds. After a while, caught in a stalemate, we simply circulated our material to the scores of national press people who slouched through the lobby on their way to another lunch of rubber chicken and canned campaign rhetoric.

A national newswire reporter chatted with us, sized up what was unfolding, and disappeared into the dining room. Ten minutes later, she returned. By this time, we had reconvened in the main hotel foyer. We were weighing our options, when the reporter informed us that she had been in the luncheon and seen two empty tables, eighteen unclaimed seats, ours. At this moment, a Mr. Battaglia, head of the Delaware Republican State Committee, asked to speak with us. He apologized profusely for the terrible mistake. We refused politely to accept his apology. Each time we refused, he ratcheted his apology up. He became profoundly sorry. We didn't accept it. He was awfully, terribly sorry. No, thank you. I stopped him by saying that we would gladly accept his apology under one condition. "What one?" He asked, brightening. "That you let some of us in to hear the rest of the candidate's speech." "That," he said, no longer apologetic, "I cannot do."

Now Mr. Battaglia's face had turned to stone. And chiseled in the stone were the words DO NOT ENTER. If we had tried to push past that face, past the security and cops, past the fresh young aide and affable hotel manager, we would have been seen as forward, aggressive, radical, even dangerous. We would have been stopped. Detained. Perhaps arrested. Made to feel that what we wanted to do that day—buy our tickets, listen to a speech, ask a question, buttonhole an aide—had been threatening and wrong.

Well, there was nothing wrong with us on this cold January day. And the more the scene unfolded, the more reporters approached us for interviews, the more stories they filed about the strange behavior of a candidate and party who claimed to seek "faith-based" solutions toward religious leaders with reserved seats—the better our team of leaders from Washington, Wilmington, Philadelphia, and New York began to feel. Local television and radio did not report on a ragtag group picketing the presidential candidate or scuffling with hotel security. No, the lead stories that afternoon described the puzzling response of the self-proclaimed proponent of faith-based initiatives, and the evening news opened with shots of two empty tables and eighteen empty chairs.

If you had been a cabdriver in Manhattan on a warm Saturday morning in June, driving north on Madison, just above 23rd Street, or a tourist out for a sunrise amble, or the Caribbean woman standing next to me waiting for a bus to take her uptown, you would have had to look twice at the scene that was unfolding.

A house had been "set" in the shadows cast by the New York Life Insurance Building. A few hours earlier, before dawn, a large trailer with a police escort had turned right off 23rd Street and headed north. The cavalcade had been met by a single person, Louise Green, a trim IAF organizer, who had waited for the trailer while the party-goers and prostitutes drifted by.

The house now sat securely on the street, supported by wooden blocks. It sat right in front of the headquarters for the New York State Democratic Party and the Gore for President Campaign. A generator hummed—powering the saws that cut the lumber that the workmen turned into steps and railings. They were finishing the front and back porches for this home. Other workers had driven the last screws into the side of the home—thirty feet wide and ten feet high—to secure a canvas sign.

The Caribbean woman studied the sign, which read:

THE INDUSTRIAL AREAS FOUNDATION ASKS:

WHERE'S AL GORE?

ON THE IMPORTANT ISSUES OF . . .

•More Affordable Nehemiah Homes and Apartments for Working Americans

•A Living Wage for All Employees of Federal Contractors and Subsidy-Users

---

The Caribbean woman held a bouquet and asked me what was happening. I described to her our six-month effort to meet with the Democratic candidate about the issues lettered on the thirty-foot-wide canvas sign attached to the side of the first floor of the Nehemiah home now located on Madison Avenue. We had contacted Senator Schumer and Tony Coelho (who had just resigned for health reasons) and his replacement, William Daley. We had received panicky calls just this week from the candidate's staff and senior people at the Democratic National Committee. Would we call off the action? Sure, we said, if we get a thirty-minute meeting with the candidate. But the candidate was busy, they whined. So were we, we said, planning this Saturday action in New York.

We had spent an enormous amount of energy setting up this unusual action. In March, at a meeting of leaders and staff, Martin Trimble had suggested transporting an entire Nehemiah home to a Manhattan location. At first, we rejected the notion. Then we all began to reconsider it, enjoying the outrageousness of the suggestion, wondering whether we could pull it off. Then we calculated the cost—for transportation, workers, and security. We met with New York City officials and received guarantees of their cooperation. There would be no placards, no whistles, no chants, and no abstract talk about housing. No, there would be a real home, to walk through, to inspect, and to tour.

The woman wished me well and boarded her bus. I remained at my station, watching the workmen complete the setup, imagining the seven hundred leaders all across the region boarding their buses, napping in vans, and catching early trains to participate in the action scheduled to start at noon. As I jotted some notes and made press calls, I saw a man charging across Madison toward me. He was short, stocky, bantam, tough talking. He claimed to represent the Democratic Party and demanded to know if we had a permit to be here. I hesitated just a bit and said, "We have all the goddamn permits anybody every issued."

"From who?" he yelled. "From where?"

"From the NYPD and anyone else you care to call."

He stalked off, grumbling over his shoulder at me, "I'm going to check upstairs." We never saw him or anyone else from the late great Democratic Party again that day.

Hours later, by half past eleven, the street had begun to fill with our leaders. Because we had taken the trouble to haul a house from our factory in the Brooklyn Navy Yard to the center of Manhattan, we had decided to show it off. Inside the home, tables were loaded with platters of fruit, cheese, crackers, vegetables, cookies, and soda. Hundreds lined up for this most unusual open house. Even the cops took a tour, checking the cabinets, peeking into the bathroom. "How much does this cost?" One of them asked. "Seventy-six thousand dollars to the buyer," said our usher, "when it's not parked on Madison Avenue. Right now, right here, it's worth about two million." The look out the back window, up Madison Avenue, was unprecedented and priceless.

Most of the leaders who toured the home and gathered their snacks were poor and working poor. Perhaps fifty already had Nehemiah homes of their own—in the South Bronx, Brooklyn, or Baltimore. Perhaps another hundred had other, larger homes of their own, in suburban Maryland or Long Island, in Center City Philadelphia or Brooklyn Heights. But the vast majority, the remaining six hundred or so, could not yet afford a home of their own. Many were immigrants from Mexico, El Salvador, and Haiti. Some were still undocumented. They had awakened at dawn in row houses in west Baltimore, southeast Washington, or north Philadelphia. They had dressed their kids and descended four stories in East Harlem tenements or East Brooklyn housing projects. They had postponed the washing, shopping, and house cleaning to join with their fellow leaders, to tour a home that was prominent in their picture of the American Dream, to participate in a public action that would have been improbable or dangerous in the countries of their birth, and to join with leaders of all races and income levels and faiths focused on clear public goals. There was a festive air inside the home and out.

At five minutes to noon, the sun bore down on the back porch stage and the street shimmered in the light. Reverend David Haberer, a Pentecostal pastor from the Rockaways in Queens who was tall and lean, with thinning red hair and the hint of a red beard, looked south down Madison at a street packed with leaders and supporters. Arnie Graf and I remained inside the home for the moment, backstage, working on last-minute preparations with the key speakers. Every few minutes, we scanned the crowd. Three photographers had appeared. One reporter. No television cameras. We worried. We had used the threat of the action to get reaction from the Gore camp—aides, staff, Jesse Jackson, Coelho, Daley, and other surrogates—but we had counted on the presence of an actual house and a large crowd to draw more media.

At noon, sharp, Reverend Haberer banged the gavel on the porch's podium and called the meeting to order. After an opening prayer, by a slight Lutheran pastor named Heidi Neumark, who served a congregation in the South Bronx with intensity and courage, fourteen leaders who represented each of the local organizations present introduced themselves and announced the turnout from each group. The rounds were lively and celebratory. While coming from different cities and sections of cities, the leaders clearly enjoyed being with one another and sharing a common organizational culture.

Start on time and end on time. Recognize yourself and one another. Hold yourself accountable ("South Bronx Churches has thirty-five leaders here today!"), so that you can demand public accountability from others and hold them to it. Take the power you build and test it against the power of others. Bring energy, joy, and irreverence to the public square, not just ideology, self-righteousness, and rote reenactments. Don't be deterred when others won't engage. Flow around the obstacles. Persist in unexpected ways.

Several speakers reminded the crowd and the large group of passersby who were observing why we were there and what we were trying to say to the two presidential candidates. Ministers and experienced leaders set the stage. But the crowd listened a little harder when three Nehemiah homeowners—one each from Brooklyn, the Bronx, and Baltimore—and living wage worker Pat Alstin spoke. Pat Alstin was not a professional speaker. She was tough, direct, no-nonsense. She had overcome enormous obstacles to get into the workforce, had found herself paid an impossibly low wage, and had fought with her fellow low-wage workers in Baltimore to pass the nation's first living wage bill. She testified simply to the impact of a better wage on her life. She communicated, just by being who she was, to the majority of those in the crowd—fellow parents, fellow workers, fellow strugglers—who had similar lives, similar pressures, similar worries, and similar limitations.

And yet, there was Pat Alston, on the porch, on the stage, speaking to the crowd. People listened even more intently to her than to some of the other more polished and more experienced speakers. You could almost read in people's eyes, "That person is just like me." And, if you looked a little deeper, you could sense the beginning of a realization, "Maybe, someday, I could do what she is doing."

The next speaker was Reverend Johnny Ray Youngblood—the individual in the IAF East Coast area who is best known. He was dressed this afternoon in a dark blue minister's shirt, without a collar, and dark slacks. He had spent his entire public life in pulpits, in front of microphones, engaging crowds, and was not at all uncomfortable on the porch of a house in the middle of Madison Avenue.

He scanned the crowd for ten seconds, then somberly said, "I have an important announcement to make." He paused. "We have learned where Al Gore is today." Another pause. Someone shouts, "Where?" Reverend Youngblood addressed the man who called out. "Al Gore is in Bal Harbor, Florida, giving a speech on Progress and Prosperity." The audience groaned, laughed.

Then Reverend Youngblood, fifty-two years old, a native of New Orleans, and a pastor of one of the most remarkable congregations in America, which he calls the "church unusual," looked up at the buildings on Madison Avenue, all sun-washed now, and began to deliver his speech:

> We are standing in the middle of a great city . . .
> At the headquarters of a once-great party . . .

In the canyons of corporate America . . .

We're here because that once-great party and its candidat
the other party and its candidate, can't seem to bring themselv
talk about the kinds of concerns that make and break our lives . . .

We're here because this booming economy, this marvel of produc
tion and wealth-creation, in the very best of times, did not solve the
problems that make and break our lives . . .

We're here because the solutions that used to be considered far
from radical—decent affordable homes, living wage work for Americans who work hard—are now not on the radar screen . . .

We're here because those of us who used to be invisible men and
invisible women are now plagued by the disappearance of opportunities—the disappearance of those common-sense rungs in the social
and economic ladder of our nation that used to be there so people
could climb up . . .

We're here because you can't climb out of poverty, you cannot, if
you can't make a living wage, if you can't buy a decent home, like the
one we are standing in today, if you can't begin building equity for
your family . . .

As he spoke, I slipped out the back door of the home and joined
the crowd. Reverend David Haberer and Ms. Avis Ransom, Arnie
Graf and Reverend Heidi Neumark flanked Reverend Youngblood as he spoke. I envied those who saw Lincoln and Douglass a
little less, as I stood with my fellow citizens and listened to the likes
of Neumark and Youngblood.

Instead of discussing and debating these self-evident truths, the candidates and their surrogates are talking about something called the
digital divide.

Now, the first time I heard about the digital divide, I looked at my
fingers and wondered if the digital divide had something to do with
the space between them.

Then I realized that the digital divide had something to do with computers and the Internet.

Then I saw photographs of the candidates in Silicon Valley, raising millions in contributions for their campaigns.

Then I began to understand the issue of the digital divide a whole lot better. The digital divide is the space between how much money Gore raises and how much money Bush raises from the new Internet millionaires.

We're gathered here today to talk about the equity divide. Just provide living wage work and the opportunity to buy one of these Nehemiah homes, and we'll order our own computers. We'll hook ourselves up. We'll go online if and when we want to.

It's the equity divide that threatens our families. It's the fact that even HUD admits that the housing situation is worsening—that more than five million American families pay half of their income for the inadequate housing, that the number of Americans paying more and more for less and less has increased by 12 percent during this boom period, and that the housing crisis is worsening.

It's the equity divide that undermines our communities. It's the fact that many of us are working two and three jobs just to make enough to survive, instead of working one living wage job. That's why we are asking the two candidates to establish a national living wage of twenty-five thousand dollars in salary and benefits for all employees of all institutions who benefit in any way form federal subsidies, tax breaks, loans, or contracts, including our own religious institutions. Stop using government money to subsidize poverty. Don't use government support to keep people out of the economic mainstream. Make contractors and financial institutions and nonprofits pay to play with federal subsidy.

It's the equity divide that we want Gore and Bush to talk about, argue about, and debate about. That's why we're here. And that's why we're having a bit of fun today by bringing this wonderful Nehemiah home to Manhattan in the city where the Nehemiah Plan began in 1983.

And that's why we'll be in Philadelphia, in July, on the night the Republicans open their convention, and that's why we'll continue this campaign long after the new president has been elected, and the banners, ads, and election props have been put away . . .

While the candidates competed with one another to give the most religious and pastoral speeches, loaded with claims to personal piety, Reverend Youngblood delivered a political speech. He didn't try to out-preach the candidates, which he could easily have done. He tried, instead, to offer a better example of what could be said and should be said *politically*. He tried to model a better and deeper brand of politics and a more engaging example of what it meant to be a "politician." The audience expressed its approval, with a long and rolling ovation. Even observers waiting at the bus stop applauded.

The one-hour action was nearly over. Fr. Marty Curtin of East Harlem took the podium. Fr. Marty was dressed in the long brown robes of his Capuchin Franciscan religious order. Tall and blond, with the face of a younger Robert Redford, he stood completely still until the crowd and street quieted. Then, in his rich, sonorous voice, he told the story of St. John the Baptist's parents, who were doubtful, unable to conceive, until blessed by the Lord. He moved seamlessly from English to Spanish, his words dominating the Manhattan canyons. There were no car horns, shouts, or squealing brakes—just the prayer of a pastor that riveted his most unlikely congregation in this most unusual place and moment of worship.

The moment reminded me of the prayer said by the Reverend John Heinemeier, in New York's City Hall, eighteen years before. A team of eight EBC leaders and allies was waiting for a crucial meeting with the mayor to begin. We stood in a hallway, just outside the mayor's office, lost in a swirl of rushing aides, shouting citizens, and argumentative staff. We were nervous, dry-mouthed, tight, that day. I sensed the tension and asked John Heinemeier to pray. He requested that we join hands, so Alice McCollum and Edgar Mendez, Fr. Powis and Reverend Youngblood, Bishop Mugavero and builder I. D. Robbins, John, and I all did.

Then Heinemeier—a rock of a minister from west Texas—bowed his head and prayed. The hallway quieted, stopped. Everyone around us either watched respectfully or bowed their heads and silently joined in. It became so quiet that Koch charged out of his office, saying, "What's going on out here." Then he saw our circle, stopped on a dime, and backed into his inner sanctum. When the prayer ended, we were calm, clear, and ready for the meeting. The decibel level rose again, and the public arena roared back to life.

That was the feel of Madison Avenue on that brilliant Saturday afternoon. A different tone, a different tenor, prevailed for about five minutes—a brief Sabbath. Then Fr. Marty finished his prayer. Reverend Haberer adjourned the meeting at 12:55. The crowd cheered.

The delegations that had traveled form Baltimore and Philadelphia boarded their buses and journeyed out to East Brooklyn, guests of the EBC leaders. There, they were treated to a Brooklyn lunch of sandwiches, salads, and cheesecake from Juniors—and were taken on a tour of the five hundred newest Nehemiah homes in the area. When the buses pulled onto the Nehemiah blocks, the leaders poured off, and homeowners stopped their gardening and kibitzing to greet them, invite them in, and regale them with stories of proud homeownership.

The key leaders who planned and participated in the action gathered in the home on Madison Avenue for an impromptu briefing led by Arnie Graf. The team felt good about the action —about the willingness to try something new, the quality of the speakers, the turnout from the local groups, and the strong response from the audience. The action had clearly worked internally. Leaders went home clearer about what we were trying to get the candidates, parties, and country to focus on. Everyone left with indelible images of the larger living realities—more affordable homes, more widespread and nonpartisan citizen participation, and more creativity in the public square—we sought to project that day. But the lack of television coverage (we learned later that the stations had sent their crews to cover a mermaid festival in Coney Island) and the generally poor response from the media in general were negatives.

Several leaders wondered whether or not we should accept the offer of a meeting with lesser Gore aides. People debated back and forth for ten minutes or so. Then Arnie proposed that we wait for two weeks and see what reactions may develop. We knew that Pulitzer Prize–winning columnist Jim Dwyer was preparing a column for the *Sunday Daily News*—bought and read by a million New Yorkers. And *Village Voice* political veteran Tom Robbins had covered the action, with a photographer in tow. Arnie ended the evaluation by praising the way the leaders worked together. Fourteen local IAF organizations, in five states and the nation's capital, over many miles and many months, had executed a smoothly run and effective joint action. In a month, they would come together again, in Philadelphia, to keep the pressure on the major candidates.

But if we had lost television cameras to the mermaids of Coney Island, how would we compete with the attractions outside the Republican National Convention? Arianna Huffington and Warren Beatty—political mermaid and merman—were floating around something called the Shadow Convention. Seattle demonstrators and economic protesters banged drums and blustered at barricades manned by the Philadelphia Police Department. A local welfare rights group led by a charismatic leader, who happened to be the sister of a movie star, successfully courted reporters searching for a sound bite.

Ceci Schickel, the driven and determined lead organizer of Philadelphia Interfaith Action, came up with a solution. Two weeks before the start of the convention, she contacted Francis X. Clines of the *New York Times* and invited him to meet with a team of Philadelphia leaders. An experienced and savvy reporter for the *Times,* a veteran of foreign wars and civil strife, Clines wasn't prepared for the fifty acres of vacant lots and sinking homes of North Philadelphia.

Clines walked the streets with Reverend Kermit Newkirk, the pastor of the one institution that remained standing in the emptiness—the Harold O. Davis Baptist Church. As they toured this urban ghost town, Clines said that the area was worse than anything he had seen—worse even than the no-man's-land in Belfast. His fine story appeared on page one of the national edition of the *Times,* with dramatic photos. It began:

> Sparing the approaching Republican Convention a civic eyesore, bulldozers are moving in on the last of the 957 sinking homes of the Logan triangle, a stricken working-class swath of North Philadelphia that has festered for more than a decade.
>
> The 80-year-old neighborhood's collapse into its own unstable landfill is stark evidence that the vaunted Philadelphia renaissance that is attracting the Republican conventioneers is at least a tale of two cities: the glittering downtown of new hotels and trendy restaurants, and frayed old working-class neighborhoods five miles to the north.
>
> Advocates for assorted causes will be arriving . . . but only Logan is offering a vivid on-site experience and eyewitness guides through a tortured saga of neighborhood blight, political promises, and bureaucratic nostrums.

Clines's piece triggered renewed interest in the local Philadelphia press. "My god," one reporter said, "you got Frank Clines to write about this!" And the international media, arriving by the hundreds, picked up on the theme. The BBC requested an interview with Reverend Newkirk. The *Toronto Star* began work on an extended story. Dutch reporters appeared at Sunday services at Harold O. Davis. A German cable company was intrigued. Logan became more than an isolated place and problem. It became a symbol of a much larger crisis—the continued burning and sinking of the major cities of the Northeast and Midwest.

On the evening of 31 July, while the Republican Convention droned on a few miles away, twelve hundred leaders from IAF organizations up and down the East Coast packed into Reverend Newkirk's church and listened to him speak with anger and passion about the reproach that was Logan.

He introduced Debbie Anderson, one of the last residents of the Logan, to tell her tale. She described how her children were startled awake at night by the sound of scavengers stripping copper and pipe from the abandoned homes on either side of hers. Her children asked her, "Mommy, mommy, will our house fall on us? Will we be killed?" She wondered whether the Republicans, whose convention theme was "leave no child behind," included her kids. "Will they come back to get mine?"

Then, Reverend Newkirk invited the Reverend Mary Laney to the pulpit. Reverend Laney was the slight and attractive Episcopal priest whose congregation was a mile away from the Logan site. She and Reverend Newkirk had become one of the most effective and feared ministerial teams in the city. Those expecting the push to come from Newkirk, who resembled an NFL lineman, were often completely bowled over when Laney applied the pressure. She gripped the sides of the pulpit and gave what we believe was the best speech of the night and the week.

One Logan—this Logan—is bad enough.

But our nation is dotted with Logans. There's another one across the river. It's called Camden. There's one just twenty-five miles to the north. Called Trenton. There's a large portion of St. Louis that looks like Logan. There's another Logan in New Orleans, where Reverend Youngblood's from. There's the infamous State Street Corridor and the other lesser West Side wastelands of Chicago. There are portions of Baltimore, of Washington, of Atlanta, of Buffalo. You name the older city or county, and you will find a version of Logan.

Now, we know better than anyone what religious institutions— congregations, synagogues, mosques—can do.

But we also know what we can't do and shouldn't do. We can't create sites for critical masses of new construction—only government can do that. We can't provide modest subsidies so that housing is affordable to working families—only government can do that. We can't force those who use federal subsidy to pay their workers a living wage—only government can do that.

I get nervous around all this talk in both parties about so-called faith-based solutions. I worry that some of those talkers are just avoiding *their* responsibilities. I'm concerned that "faith-based" is a code word for "no cost."

We won't fall for any of that. BEING A PERSON OF FAITH DOESN'T MEAN YOU'RE EASY TO FOOL.

When she finished, the choir, on fire, began singing "America the Beautiful." The crowd, turning to leave, picked up the song without prompting. The singing was loud, deep, heartfelt, almost startling. We sang what we felt and lived, what we worked for and organized for—for God's grace on Logan, on Debbie Anderson and her kids, and on all the frightened children of the nation this night. We sang that the nation's undeniable good be finally crowned with brotherhood.

Still singing, the crowd surged into the streets for one of the most unusual processions in the history of the city. With television helicopters circling beneath dark and roiling clouds, twelve hundred people paraded past abandoned blocks whose grass has been cut and weeds trimmed to look good for the visiting media, past rows of abandoned buildings that had been much reduced by frantic demolition crews, finally to the last forlorn cluster of homes occupied by the Anderson family and others.

We did well that night on the local news stations. First they reported on the Republicans. Then they covered us. The most watched program ended with the reporter mentioning the "somber irony" of the singing of "America the Beautiful," with shots of the crowd, with a portion of the powerful singing. We appreciated the fact that he had noticed. But there was nothing ironic about it.

We pressed forward through the remainder of the election season—and well beyond. Long after the banners and bunting were packed away, in the spring of 2001, Mayor John Street of Philadelphia, a former antagonist, announced his complete support for a blight removal strategy based on our recommendations. In the winter of 2002, the consistently uncooperative new mayor of Baltimore followed suit. Like "Nehemiah" and "living wage," "blight removal" was beginning to enter the national vocabulary.

But we never did meet with either of the two major candidates. And we learned that we had a long way to go before we could initiate and sustain the same kinds of complex public relationships with national figures as we had with local leaders. These relationships can't be captured on a poster, in a cartoon, or even on a television screen. They take time to achieve and time to describe. This is the story of one such relationship, in a fairly large "local" arena—New York City.

CHAPTER 7

Ambiguity, Reciprocity, Victory

On 3 April 2000, another lovely morning in lower Manhattan, in the period that will always lie on the other side of the divide left by the destruction of the World Trade Center, a small team of veteran leaders slowly gathered. We brought our cups of coffee and tea to the twenty-first floor of 74 Trinity Place, one block south of the Trade Center, to the headquarters of the Trinity Grants Program. An elegant library occupied one end of the floor—about four hundred square feet of wood paneling, packed shelves, and stained glass. The view out the west windows included the Hudson River, sparkling this morning, and the Jersey City waterfront. The windows facing east provided glimpses of the crowded canyons of Wall Street. It was a normal business day in New York, but not at all a normal political day.

A round, wooden table dominated the center of the room. Reverend Johnny Ray Youngblood settled into a chair, along with two of his talented associates, Reverend David Brawley and Ron Hudson. Reverend Getulio Cruz arrived, after dropping his son off at a lower Manhattan public school. Reverend Cruz—in his mid-

thirties, the father of two—led a Hispanic Pentecostal congregation on the lower East Side. Unlike many of his fellow Pentecostal
ministers, he participated fully and enthusiastically in the public
issues of his community and city. Reverend Heidi Neumark com-
muted by subway from the South Bronx. Another South Bronx
leader, a tall, serious Episcopal priest named Bert Bennett, also
settled in. Fr. Marty Curtin rushed in, just ahead of Msgr. John
Powis. Msgr. Powis, in his mid-sixties, was the senior member of
this very experienced leadership team. He now served a dynamic
and demanding parish in Bushwick after a twenty-five-year stint
in Oceanhill-Brownsville. He had experienced his baptism by fire
in the bitter and racially charged Oceanhill-Brownsville school
controversy in the late sixties—which pitted local supporters of
community control against the leaders and allies of the United
Federation of Teachers.

Another controversy threatened to consume the city, and we
were meeting to finalize plans for a discussion with one of the
main players in that controversy, Mayor Giuliani, later that morning. Undercover officers had shot and killed an unarmed security
guard, Patrick Dorismond, during a scuffle in front of a midtown
bar. The facts were confused and conflicting. Advocates rushed to
link this shooting to the killing of Amadou Diallo, the unarmed
African salesman shot in the vestibule of his building by four
plainclothes officers just a year before, and the brutal assault on
Abner Louima in a Brooklyn precinct house. The mayor reacted
by asking the public to be patient, then by defending the police,
and then by questioning the character of the dead man.

We knew we were moving on very dangerous ground. One rail
that ran through this terrain was the primal need for safety. In
most of our organizations, from the very first individual meeting,
training session, or house meeting, people talked about how violence and street crime warped their lives—when and if they held

evening meetings, where they walked and shopped, what subway stations they used and avoided, what schools they sent their children to, the very survival of those children, especially their young men, and, most especially, young black men.

In one of the first EBC house meetings I attended in East New York, in 1981, I arrived on Bradford Street only to find the street blocked off by sawhorses and a resident standing guard. The resident recognized me, pulled one of the sawhorses back, and let me pass. I could see that the other end of the street was also blocked off and guarded. "What's up?" I asked. The unofficial guard told me that the only way to persuade everyone to come to the house meeting was to guarantee security. "Otherwise," the affable resident said, "we all go home to nothing, and we'll never meet again." In the packed meeting that took place that night, person after person described the lives of insecurity and terror they led.

The second rail was the ongoing concern about police performance and responsiveness. Often, in 1981 and throughout the eighties, the police just weren't there. And when they were present, it was sometimes worse. Police would hail a middle-aged African American walking home from work this way, "Hey, n_____, we want to talk to you." Thousands of harsh words, hard looks, stops and searches, illegal entries, corrupt practices by rogue cops like Michael Dowd (who admitted his guilt in testimony before the latest high-profile investigation of improper police behavior conducted by the Mollen Commission), and slow responses to domestic crises—the drip-drip-drip of disrespect and insensitivity and worse—had created a painful knot of distrust and distaste within the very people who needed the cops the most.

This real and psychic terrain was—and is—the American equivalent of the Balkans. It is a place of currents and undertows, of blood feuds and growing grudges, of real slights and innocent mistakes, of incidents decades old that feel as fresh and immediate as the evening news. It is a landscape crowded with demagogues and apologists, tyrants and opportunists, romantics and double agents. It demands a writer capable of producing great literature, superb travel reporting, top-flight political science, sociology and psychology, a knowledge of religious and culture history, and the right mix of objective distance and personal empathy. America needs a new Rebecca West, who, right before World War II, poured all of her powers of intelligence and insight and wit into the more than eleven hundred pages of her monumental work, *Black Lamb and Grey Falcon.* That graphic guide to Croatia, Serbia, Bosnia, and beyond is as useful and relevant today as it was more than sixty years ago.

But there was no Rebecca West to guide us—just very high anxiety, activists accusing, cops reacting, a large cast of public players reprising roles from earlier crises, and a mayor who, to put it mildly, kept proving that he lacked a feel and an ear for the complex reactions of black and Hispanic New Yorkers. So we thought that we would try to detail those reactions, the expressions of pain and fury and despair our ministers and leaders heard every hour of every day, face to face, directly to the mayor, in depth. We knew him well enough to understand that we would be jeopardizing our public relationship with him. This relationship had developed fitfully over a period of fifteen years. It had become, strangely and unexpectedly, a very productive relationship. The production could be seen, felt, and measured—in the number of homes built, streets paved, police response sharpened, parks improved, and public housing projects cleaned and secured—in communities that had long been ignored. And it would all be at risk in an hour or so, when we walked up the steps of City Hall, for our meeting with him.

The Rudy Giuliani we first met in 1986 was a machine-busting, mob-busting United States attorney who had captured the attention of the entire media establishment—from right to left. He looked, sounded, and acted unlike any public figure in the region at the time. He made the unindicted machine hacks and graying Village progressives look like wax figures in a museum of political types—bloodless, colorless, and motionless.

We sought him out because we found ourselves in a situation that demanded the attention of Giuliani the law enforcement officer, not Giuliani the emerging politician. Our East Brooklyn organization was building hundreds of homes a year in Brownsville at the time. A major trade union began to pressure our builder to make contributions to the union's health and pension funds. The union representative handed our builder a list of thirty ghost workers and told him to make the payments in their names. The union fellow politely explained that he would then spread the money around to the other unions involved. In return, we would have "peace" on our construction site. We already had "peace" on our site, so we told the fellow, also politely, that we did not plan to make any payments.

A few weeks later, more than a dozen guys from the local came to our office and trooped up the narrow stairs of our model home. I. D. Robbins, our peppery and savvy builder, and I sat across the table from the union crew. They hadn't made themselves clear, they said. They needed to make us understand how things worked around New York. They were even giving us a better deal because we were with "the churches." In fact, the president of their union had just been named man of the year by Catholic Charities, so we were really all on the same team.

Robbins listened and then told them that we couldn't afford to pay anything, not for one ghost worker, much less thirty, not a penny. He told them we wanted a break, a pass, and that we wouldn't tell a soul if they gave us one. The key union rep got exercised. We didn't seem to get it. They had *already* given us a break. And they were offering us a discount. And there was no way they could let someone get by without paying. How would that look to everyone else in Brooklyn? And, besides, who the hell did we think we were going to tell, anyway? These often-bizarre negotiations continued, over several meetings, for many hours, with members of their team sometimes whining about how we were making them look bad, sometimes threatening us with tales about what the unfortunate accidents could occur if we didn't resolve what they called a "labor dispute."

Robbins didn't give an inch. So the local started to picket us. This was the first time we had been picketed at all, much less for not agreeing to respond to a shakedown. A drowsy union rep sat in a folding chair near our office and held up a sign if anyone happened to look his way. No other union worker stopped working. The homes kept rising on block after block. The only people upset by this action were a few progressives and liberals who visited us and couldn't understand why we weren't more mortified by this labor crisis.

Then the phone calls started. At first, the callers were just gruff and abusive—not much worse than a normal New York phone conversation. Then, they promised to kill someone connected with our efforts. Then, the calls began to come to our homes. That's when we went to the U.S. attorney and described what was going on.

All the qualities Giuliani has demonstrated throughout his public life—a feel and an ear for a crisis involving corruption or crime or terrorism, an appetite for the details of a situation, a quick commitment of resources to respond to the crisis, and a determination to follow up and follow through—were evident almost immediately. In fact, his office had already launched an investigation of the union threatening us, based on complaints from other builders and groups.

This was encouraging—but only up to a point. The pressure

kept increasing. The president of the union called for a final negotiation. Our team met and decided that two Roman Catholic
priests were best suited for this session in Manhattan. Our thinking was fairly shallow at this stage: the union president was a major
Roman Catholic figure; the mob seemed reluctant to harm Roman
Catholic clergy; and the U.S. attorney's team was closing in. This
analysis made sense to everyone but the two priests picked for the
mission. "What," one of them asked, "if we were *wrong*?"

On the morning of meeting, the priests went dutifully off on
their assignment. I hadn't read the *Times* that morning, and neither had they. As they later described it, they arrived at the local's
plush headquarters and were warmly greeted by another top union
officer. The president and secretary-treasurer were unexpectedly
tied up, they were told, and he would be happy to speak with them.
He offered coffee and Danish. He asked how things were going in
the parishes. He talked in a loud and clear voice—very loud and
very clear—about how much he loved the Nehemiah effort, loved
the churches, and loved to think that his men were building such
fine homes for the working poor. Our two priests began to relax.
This went on for twenty minutes. No threats. No last offers. No
pressure. Finally, one of the priests asked, "Isn't there anything else
you would like to say?" The union official expressed dismay, "Why,
no, I just wanted to tell you, on behalf of my local, how much we
love the Nehemiah Plan." He addressed his comments directly
toward the middle of their chests, where, he must have assumed, a
wire was recording every word.

When they reached the street, the priests raced for the first pay
phone. Their relief and surprise surged through the line. "It's a
miracle!" they said. "You wouldn't believe it. There must have been
some misunderstanding somewhere." I asked if they had seen a
newspaper. They hadn't. A *Times* headline announced that the
U.S. attorney's office had indicted two union officials for shaking
down other construction sites in the city.

A year or so later, in the months leading up to the 1989 mayoral election, the leaders of our three organizations in New York City at the time—East Brooklyn Congregations, the Queens Citizens Organization, and South Bronx Churches—met with both Giuliani and David Dinkins. We asked each candidate to agree to meet individually with fifteen leaders—five in each borough—in the home, apartment, or parish house of the leader. We believed that the candidates would get a better sense of us and that we would get a much better sense of them in these face-to-face, one-to-one sessions. And we asked each candidate to attend a public account-ability assembly, of about one thousand leaders, near the end of the campaign.

During this period, other aspects of both men's characters emerged. Giuliani the candidate seemed less focused, more dis-tracted and reactive, than Giuliani the prosecutor. One afternoon, we met him in a pizza parlor across the street from the Cathedral of St. John the Divine in Manhattan. Richard Green, the African-American chancellor of New York City Public Schools, had died suddenly of asthma. Giuliani agreed to meet after the funeral for thirty minutes to be briefed about the individual meetings he had agreed to do and the assembly coming up.

The candidate arrived, tailed by an aide who carried a cell phone so active it seemed to be smoking. The aide was short, breathless, and wired. Giuliani seemed intense as well. His knee kept pumping up and down under the table, as we talked. The aide whispered that the *Times* was on the line, pressing for the candi-date's position on Northern Ireland. We were trying to get him to focus on more local issues, like crime, affordable housing, and poorly performing public schools. We would talk minute or two, then the phone would ring. The aide would answer, listen, whisper into Giuliani's ear. Giuliani asked about the assembly. The aide hissed, "The *Times*." Giuliani's knee would pump a little faster. He would simultaneously try to talk about the assembly and jot notes on a napkin. The word "Ireland" stood out in the middle of his scrawl.

We asked why the hell he had to come up with "a position" on Northern Ireland when he didn't even have one on how to produce homes and apartments in New York. Giuliani turned to his aide and started to ask him, "Yeah, why." The aide shot back, "Because there are lots of Irish in the city and because it's the *Times*." By then, the candidate was scribbling more notes. The notes were becoming a statement of some sort. And the statement was not about housing in New York.

In the most improbable of all outcomes, Giuliani followed through on his commitment to meet individually with fifteen leaders, and his opponent, Dinkins, did not. We would pick him up early in the morning, drive him out to Bushwick, the South Bronx, or Southeast Queens, and drop him off at his first appointment. He would be alone, without aides and cell phones, without press releases and media attention—a middle-aged white man in a suit walking into Hope Gardens Housing Project to meet for a half an hour with EBC leader Alberta Williams. There, he learned about life in public housing and on the treacherous streets of Bushwick. And Alberta Williams would learn about what made this man think he could be a more effective mayor than his opponent. To this day, he remains the only public official who took the time to do individual meetings with leaders like Reverend Youngblood and Reverend Haberer, Reverend Neumark and Pat Oettinger, Woody Head and Fr. Grange.

Then, just as improbably, he did not attend the accountability event that we sponsored. It was then that we noticed another trait in his public character—a tendency to fade completely and unpredictably out of a relationship for extended periods of time. We never imagined or assumed that we were close to either him or Dinkins. We weren't even interested in the kind of partisan, personal, friendly, first-name relationship that many others sought. He was never "Rudy" to our leaders, just as Dinkins was never called "David." We wanted a more public relationship, where there was mutual respect, mutual understanding, some agreement, some disagreement, and the right amounts of tension and formality, engagement and distance. For long stretches, we *had* that kind of relationship. And then we simply didn't.

While Giuliani disappeared in the weeks before the election, Dinkins, who refused to do the individual meetings, decided to attend the assembly. Our leaders packed the basement of St. Paul the Apostle Church, right across the street from Fordham's Manhattan campus. When Dinkins arrived, the assembly had already started and Reverend Youngblood was speaking. Dinkins, impatient and grouchy, paced in the sanctuary and told one of the organizers, "Tell that preacher to stop." No one told Reverend Youngblood any such thing. Youngblood concluded, and Dinkins, the first serious African American candidate for mayor, received an unexpected standing ovation when he appeared on the stage and approached the podium. Then he gave a long and dreadful speech, lecturing the audience on technical issues of housing policy, not seeming to know where he was or whom he was addressing. By the end of his remarks, many of the same people who stood and applauded sat on their hands, even quietly booed.

Dinkins won the 1989 election by forty thousand votes. He proceeded to govern the city in much the same way he behaved at our assembly—imperiously at times, distractedly at times, quickly squandering the deep racial and ethnic pride that he embodied, and talking technically in settings and at times that demanded a more political and relational touch. Four years later, he lost to Giuliani by about the same number of votes, in part because those who cheered him early in his first term had grown disgruntled and disappointed by election day in 1993. They simply stayed home.

For the first two years of Giuliani's initial term, we worked reasonably well together. He strongly supported the continuation of the Nehemiah effort. In fact, when his first housing commissioner, who did not value Nehemiah, secretly cut the budget appropriation designated for affordable home construction, we called for a meeting with the mayor. He agreed immediately, scheduled a meeting the day after our call, summoned the commissioner, and ordered her, in our presence, to reinstate the funding. We had an adequate, working, public relationship with the city administration—direct access to the mayor, direct access to all commissioners, and direct answers, sometimes satisfactory and sometimes not, to reasonable requests.

That relationship began to fray in 1995. We were meeting many people, through our congregations and elsewhere, who were doing city work as employees of private contractors. They were security guards, food service workers, clerical workers, janitors, and data entry people. The contractors paid them minimum wage, with no benefits, and pocketed large profits. Our sister organization in Baltimore had already authored and passed the nation's first living wage bill. We decided to see if the mayor would agree to negotiate a living wage standard into the contracts that the city was signing with various service providers.

We held three hourlong meetings with the mayor and his top aides on this matter. We went to great lengths to describe the real cost of low wages—in public assistance needed by these low-wage workers simply to survive, in higher turnover and reduced productivity, and in the necessity to work two or three jobs to feed and support a family. The workers themselves, decent, moderate, and hardworking, spoke for themselves in these sessions. The mayor and his staff listened, but disagreed. Each meeting became tighter and grimmer. By the end of the third session, it was clear that we were getting nowhere and that the mayor could not believe that we would take this issue on.

We found an unlikely ally in the City Council—maverick Bay Ridge councilman Sal Albanese, who had already begun to discuss a living wage bill. Albanese could not have been more isolated and more marginal in a council totally controlled by speaker Peter Vallone. Because Albanese refused to toe the Vallone line, he had no chairmanship, no perks, and no status in the council. He did have a relationship with Kevin McCabe, Vallone's no-nonsense chief of staff and the second most powerful person in the council universe. So we began to meet with McCabe and Albanese and designed a limited living wage bill that Vallone decided he could support.

When the bill was introduced, with hundreds of our leaders present, the mayor counterattacked. First, several deputies told the media that Metro IAF seemed to want to turn the clock back and rebuild the Berlin Wall—another not so subtle attempt to say that we were socialists. Then, a reporter asked the mayor why he was fighting with Reverend Youngblood and Metro IAF, "Wasn't Metro IAF a sacred cow?" Giuliani said, "Sacred cows make the best hamburger meat."

It was a wonderful, all-out, New York political brouhaha. In July of 1996, the City Council overwhelmingly passed a modified bill by a vote of forty-one to seven. The mayor promptly and loudly vetoed it. We organized more support, derided the mayor's veto, and kept pushing. The council then overrode his veto by an even greater margin. It took the city comptroller six months to work out the prevailing wage figures for each of the categories covered. But eventually the contract workers received raises of anywhere from three to five dollars an hour. The mayor remained unreconciled. The lines to City Hall went dead in 1996. No mayoral aide answered or returned a single phone call. Most of the formerly responsive commissioners stopped responding. Some went on the offensive against us: the housing commissioner at the time cut all future funding to a seven-hundred-house Nehemiah phase planned for an area called Spring Creek, citing "environmental concerns." A few commissioners sent back-channel messages: they would meet with us only if we agreed to meet off-site, without media, and with absolutely no leaking of this to the mayor and his minions.

We had known, when we decided to champion the living wage bill, that one casualty of the campaign could be our relationship with the mayor. Clearly, the concept of a government-determined wage standard clashed with the mayor's free-market views. The merits, which we had painstakingly detailed, did not matter here as well. We decided the passage of the bill, the potential impact on the lives of the workers involved, and the signal that successful legislation in New York would send to other municipalities made the risk worth taking. We didn't know that the freeze-out would deepen and last several years. And we had no idea how, or if, the freeze-out would end. But we believed we would find a way to force the mayor back into the relationship, or there would come a day when he would see the need to renew his relationship with us.

That day came—suddenly, unexpectedly, violently, terribly— when four police officers shot Amadou Diallo in the vestibule of his apartment building in the Bronx.

The killing polarized the city. Reverend Al Sharpton quickly established himself as the focal point for the large number of New Yorkers who sought to respond to the shooting. Religious and civic leaders who rarely or grudgingly associated with Sharpton took part in the daily protests and expressions of civil disobedience. Others sided with the mayor, called for patience and prayer, or remained silent. Our own leaders and members were outraged by the incident, but felt trapped. If we participated institutionally, as Metro IAF, in the growing protests we would be throwing our support behind a strategy—ritual protests, ritual gatherings, a ten-point plan that had no chance of being implemented, and demonization of the mayor and all police—that we knew would fail and that ran counter to our best instincts of how to create lasting and meaningful change in the city.

On the other hand, if we did not act, we would be ignoring the deep pain and anger of the vast majority of the members of our congregations and associations. The followers of Reverend Youngblood and Fr. Grange, of Irving Domenech and Maria Nieves, of Marty Curtin and Bert Bennett, wanted their leaders, and Metro IAF, to do *something*.

But what? We had long discussions and arguments, through two evening meetings, involving twenty top leaders, until we came to two conclusions. Any individual or institution that wanted to participate in the ongoing protests should feel totally free to do so. But Metro IAF, collectively, would seek to carve out a third position in the city—not supportive of the mayor and not supportive of Sharpton's response—but rooted in our own sense of what needed to be done to improve the recruitment of more minority officers and the response of the NYPD to legitimate local complaints about police behavior, attitude, and response. And we would seek a meeting with the mayor to see where he now stood.

In mid-February of 1999, with the intensity level rising, the demonstrations growing, and the mayor increasingly isolated, we called the one figure in the city who knew the mayor well, knew us well, and spoke to both—Herman Badillo. Seven minutes after we called Badillo, asking him if he thought the mayor would want to meet, Badillo called back. He had spoken to the mayor. The mayor did want to meet. The sooner the better.

On 22 February, a top team of Metro IAF leaders, New York citizens—Reverend Youngblood and Alberta Williams, Msgr. Peyton and Fr. Curtin, Reverend Neumark and Reverend Cruz, Ann Scott and Betty Turner, Reverend Patrick O'Connor and Reverend John Vaughn—trooped into City Hall for a meeting with the mayor. In the distance, two blocks away, demonstrators were chanting in front of police headquarters. Security at City Hall was even tighter than usual. And we were tight, tense, worried that either someone in the mayor's camp or someone in the anti-mayor camp might have tipped off the media about this delicate meeting.

Reverend Youngblood opened the meeting by recognizing Herman Badillo, who had served as an honest broker for this session. Then Reverend Youngblood addressed the mayor, who was on time, focused, and a little tense himself. A simple written agenda had been placed in front of the mayor. It read:

1. Rounds and Introductions
2. Metro IAF Expectations of a Renewed Working Relationship with City Hall and City Agencies
3. Mayor Giuliani's Expectations of a Renewed Working Relationship with Metro IAF
4. Specific Issues—Housing, Police, Education, Regular Working Meetings and Access to Commissioners
5. Next Meeting Date

Reverend Youngblood explained that, throughout our twenty-five-year history in the city, beginning with Ed Koch, we had always had tension with mayors, as well as many moments of common agreement. We were not looking for anything special or different—renewed access to the mayor, regular meetings with commissioners, a professional pattern of responses to our requests, public recognition when things went well, public criticism when they did not, and no ambushes by either side. Reverend Youngblood presented this quietly, matter-of-factly, and directly. Giuliani looked up from the agenda and said, "That sounds all right to me." Then Reverend Youngblood asked the mayor what his expectations were. And the mayor said, "The same." The room was quiet. We had not asked him to explain his reasons for trying to relegate us to political Siberia—much less ask him for an apology we knew he would never give. He did not ask us why we had launched a living wage campaign that led to an embarrassing public defeat for him and his administration. Nor did he ask us for an apology he knew we would never offer.

The mayor just said, "The same." And we then began to do public business on a wide range of complex and thorny issues—including how to recruit more minority officers for the NYPD. The mayor never tried to use the fact that we were meeting as a weapon in his ongoing public battle with Reverend Sharpton. Reverend Sharpton never tried to criticize Reverend Youngblood and the other Metro IAF leaders for meeting with Mayor Giuliani. In one of the most polarized and complex moments in recent New York political history, our leaders had managed to stake out a third position in the city and to renew a productive relationship with a mayor and an administration whose actions and decisions had impact on the daily lives of many poor and working poor New Yorkers.

That renewed relationship translated into tangible gains. We kept building hundreds of the most affordable homes in the city in East Brooklyn and the South Bronx (for the record, Giuliani never tried to *stop* our ongoing efforts; his commissioner had pulled the plug on any future work). The "environmental issues" proved to be minor, and the funding for the seven hundred homes we planned to build at Spring Creek was restored. We persuaded the administration to invest in the upgrade of the forgotten park areas along the East River in lower Manhattan. Teams of leaders from public housing projects in the South Bronx and upper and lower Manhattan pressed for improved response from the housing authority on a wide range of concerns, and began to receive it. The mayor asked our groups to help recruit thousands of children for an expanded health care program called HealthStat, and we enthusiastically agreed. On Sundays, poor families lined up outside rectories and church basements in Washington Heights, Bushwick, and the lower East Side to sign up for health coverage. We worked with the NYPD to recruit more minority officers and kept the pressure on the department to continue to crack down on rampant drug activity in many of our areas. Working with the mayor, we attacked the bloated and corrupt bilingual education establishment in the Board of Education and forced a reluctant chancellor to agree to an aggressive reform package. On issue after issue, in agency after agency, affecting scores of communities, our organized teams of leaders learned what it was like when a focused government actually *wanted* to respond to focused citizens.

Now, a little more than a year later, in March of 2000, there's another incident, another police shooting. There's another young, black man, Patrick Dorismond, lying dead in the street. There's another outcry. There's another time of intense racial strife.

When it's a quarter of nine on a Monday morning, and the city is inflamed, and you are preparing to meet with a mayor who has made some terrible errors in judgment . . .

When you realize that most people can't get a meeting with this mayor, and it is a risk in itself just to *have* the meeting, because those in the hate-the-mayor-camp may decide to turn on you . . .

When you know that the mayor has recommitted to a whole series of practical strategies that have already benefited scores of thousands of people and could benefit many more for decades to come . . .

When all that, and more, is in the political mix, *that's* when you realize that you are going to earn your money that day.

Over the weekend, I have spoken with almost every person gathering in the library this morning, testing some ideas on them, getting their thoughts, trying to sense how much risk we all are up for. By the time we sit down, we have the outline of an approach, and I lay it out for discussion and revision.

We start by trying to pinpoint *why* we are doing this and who we are—collectively, not individually—when we walk through the doors of City Hall in little more than an hour. We're not reacting to the mayor. We're not reacting to the media—or seeking the media's attention this time. We're not there to support or undercut the anti-Giuliani crowd in the city. We have absolutely no interest in how this all "plays" in the senatorial race between the mayor and Hillary Rodham Clinton.

No, we're preparing for this meeting because so many members of our congregations have approached pastors and fellow leaders and said, in so many words, "Do something. Try something. Make some sense of all of this." We're there for ourselves—because we have had a significant role in the recent history of police performance, crime reduction, and revitalizing neighborhoods. We consider ourselves active players in the great, complex drama of the city. And we are here because we sense, today, that months or years from now, people will have a right to ask what is it that we did in this time and place. But what can we *do* an hour from now, a mile away, across the table from this mayor?

After planning our strategy, we debate whether or not to raise with him the threat to the future of police work in the city that this latest incident has contributed to and how best to preserve the real achievements of his administration, of his two very different police chiefs, and of the men and women of the NYPD. We are among the few groups that value the work of the police, appreciate the improvements in public safety and police response in the Giuliani years, and yet deplore his handling of the Dorismond matter. If the department reverts to its pre-Giuliani state, then more of our people get killed and hurt; our homeowners and tenants stop taking evening walks; and the drug dealers reassert their hold on more blocks and buildings. If the mayor doesn't demonstrate that he understands the concerns of the vast majority of moderate New Yorkers and doesn't move to correct the imbalances that lead to tragic incidents, he will expose his most important achievement to dismantling.

This situation requires laser surgery. On all sides, we see antagonists armed with mallets.

More or less ready, more nervous than usual, we walk the six long blocks to City Hall. It's a quarter of ten now. The markets have opened, but the streets are still packed with people—and memories. So much of New York's early history, as described in the wonderful tome, *Gotham,* occurred in these blocks south of Canal. The wild, old mix of Dutch and English and Indians and slaves, of traders and farmers, servants and trappers, is long gone. We walk past some of their graves, in the cemeteries of Trinity Church.

Three centuries later, there's a new mix of stock traders and bankers, janitors and secretaries, e-commerce entrepreneurs and sidewalk salesmen, professional pols and citizen leaders, all pounding the same pavement, in a city that manufactures excess and tragedy on an operatic scale.

We hustle across Broadway and cut through City Hall Park, now beautifully restored, where seventeenth-century transgressors were often tortured and hanged. I mention this to our team. Gallows humor. No one laughs for very long. Reverend Youngblood asks me for the third time to review the remarks he has composed for the start of the meeting. He is usually more at ease before a session with a powerful opponent or ally. We rehearse it as we climb the steps of City Hall and head for the door.

Thirty years, ago, a college classmate named Andy Miceli said that he always felt a rush of excitement—a thrill—when he entered City Hall. It was a funny thing to say at the time—in 1970, at Yale, when the symbols of the establishment were either literally under siege or the easy targets of our unearned cynicism. Andy was an old-fashioned kid—an Italian, a New Yorker, an enthusiast. I never forgot the *way* he said what he said. His voice seemed charged—with wonder, with respect, with something close to love for this place.

I'm not sure we feel the same thrill. But I can say that this City Hall—nestled in a park, near Hart Crane's bridge ("thy cables breathe the North Atlantic still . . ."), surrounded by congested streets, but safe and stolid and tranquil on its base of block and steps—stirs us. The city halls of Chicago, Philadelphia, and Baltimore simply don't compare—in the same way that no other lakefront compares to Chicago's, no other harbor matches Baltimore's, and few other historic areas compete with Philly's Society Hill.

When you enter New York's City Hall, you enter a special place—no matter who sits in the mayor's quarters to the left, or who occupies the speaker's offices to the right, or who trudges up the central staircase to the City Council chambers on the second floor. The place feels bigger and grander than anyone who ever inhabited it—although La Guardia came close to filling it, as did Giuliani in the weeks after 11 September. Like the White House, this City Hall seems to loom over those who work there and those who come there to do what we believe to be the most exciting business of all—the public's business.

That's the business we're here to do today—four African Americans, one Hispanic, four whites; eight men and one woman; seven religious professionals and two laypeople; eight volunteers and one paid organizer; two native New Yorkers and seven born and raised in other parts of the nation or the state.

As soon as we file through the metal detector, we are ushered upstairs to the conference room on the second floor where we have met the mayor many times before. A huge, round table—perhaps twelve feet in diameter—dominates the center of the room. Wide, high windows in the south and west walls admit as much light as the morning has to offer. Photos of the mayor and his family crowd the mantel above the fire escape. You have the sense that a child might roller-skate into the room at any moment.

We take our seats—nine of the dozen leather chairs arrayed around the table, with Reverend Youngblood in the center and four of us on either side of him—and wait. The mayor arrives almost as soon as we settle in, followed by Deputy Mayor Tony Coles, who helped coordinate this meeting and who is the person at City Hall we have had the most productive relationship with.

The game plan, which Reverend Youngblood and I reviewed just a few minutes before, was for him to thank the mayor for his time and outline the three larger pieces of the meeting, as we saw it, before starting the rounds. Reverend Youngblood skipped from the thank-you to the rounds, with nothing in between. Luckily, the first person to introduce himself—Fr. Curtin—took a deep breath and told his story about the youth group very well. Then Heidi Neumark spoke. Then Reverend David Brawley. Then Reverend Getulio Cruz. By the time the rounds worked their way back to Reverend Youngblood, he was clear, focused, and took charge of the first part of the meeting, as we had planned.

Each leader told a powerful story—and told it well. Each story was short, specific, not overstated or overdrawn, and crisply concluded. Each person spoke 60, 90, or 120 seconds and then stopped. Ending a story or vignette is like nailing a dive. There's no splash, no smack of skin on water. The body seems to evaporate as it enters the pool. All that remains is the memory of the diver. When a story ends well, there's nothing left but the picture of women praying in a small Lutheran church, crying as they pray, because they fear their sons could be shot by cops.

After the rounds, which take nearly fifteen minutes, Reverend

Youngblood talks about the two profound contexts of the current crisis—the reality of death and the inescapable reality of another young black man lifeless in the street. The mayor sits forward, makes only a comment or two, grimly listens to our grim tales.

When Reverend Youngblood finishes his short remarks, he asks the mayor to give us his view of what has happened in the city and why.

Giuliani begins to speak quietly, clearly, directly. There is no ferocity, no contempt, no ridicule, none of the Roman Catholic high school smart aleck quality sometimes present when he feels under siege or when he hears criticism from those he doesn't respect. He's listened to our stories. He's not overreacting. He's taking his time to lay out his case—starting slowly and carefully.

He talks about the context as he sees it—a series of three, very different incidents. The first is the Louima incident. "This was a crime, a depraved act, committed by at least one police officer." He points out that the blue wall of silence collapsed here. "Commissioner Safir transferred the entire precinct. And officers began to talk."

The second incident was the Diallo shooting—"clearly a mistake, a terrible mistake, either an innocent mistake, or a negligent mistake, or a criminal mistake." The word "mistake" is repeated again and again, as if he wants us to understand that he believes that the Diallo incident should never have happened, would never have happened, if the police involved had performed professionally.

The third incident is the Dorismond shooting. He tells us that he cannot discuss several facts relating to this case. But he believes that, in this instance, the police responded professionally and properly. Additional facts, new witnesses, future revelations will lead many in the city to the same conclusion, he predicts. In the middle of this discussion, he searches his inside suit coat pocket for a piece of paper. Not finding it, he asks Tony Coles to get it from his office downstairs.

He has laid out the framework for his argument, and he is warming to it now. For a total of twenty minutes, with Coles now back and the chart in front of him, he reviews all of the facts that he has tried to present in recent weeks—the reduction in police shootings overall, the dramatic difference in use of force in his administration versus the Dinkins administration, and the relative restraint of the NYPD in comparison to most other big city departments.

As he speaks, I recall a meeting with Police Commissioner Robert McGuire, in 1983 or so. He was very weary the day we met him—having come from a long meeting on internal affairs investigations. We asked him how things were going, before we went into our agenda. He sighed and said, "Oh, all right, I suppose, except for the five hundred cops who have made threats against me." Then, he caught himself, shifted gears—a decent, tired, worn man working hard to manage a mixed and sometimes-renegade force.

And I think about how the cops I grew up with in Chicago—in what used to be called a "cop" neighborhood—viewed their jobs. They resented the blacks and Hispanics (the "mutts," they sometimes called them) they had to deal with. They hated the pols they had to rescue from bar fights, domestic disputes, and whorehouses in the middle of the night, so that not a hint of scandal appeared. They sneered at the good government types who were always squealing for reform. And they despised the community activists who demanded that they patrol the streets, for Chrissake, instead of working their second or third jobs or drinking in the loading bay of a local warehouse.

And I remember the cops a mild-mannered woman religious and I tried to "train" in better community relations in Jersey City. The training took place in a bleak and isolated barracks, just a few hundred yards from the harbor shore, perhaps a mile from the Statue of Liberty. One red-headed sergeant stood up right in the middle of my attempt to instruct disgruntled cadets in the value of public relationships. He marched down the aisle of the classroom toward me. He stopped, too close to me, right in my face, and glared. He said, "I've been trying to think what you are." In the background, the forty or so white officers growled, hooted, and cheered. The only three black cadets, sitting side by side, kept their eyes straight down, as if reading the notes they hadn't taken. The sergeant shared his revelation: "I know you. I know what you are. You're a lion-tamer. You're came here to try to tame the lions. And to force us to work with dysfunctionals." The whites went wild. 'But—it—ain't—gonna—work." The crowd roared. The blacks didn't move a muscle. I soldiered on for a few minutes more, gathered up my notes, and made sure the sister and I got the hell out of there.

So, as we listen to the mayor, we don't take for granted what it means to make cops behave in a more restrained way. In fact, we don't take anything for granted. And we don't doubt many of the mayor's facts. He's done his research. This is as big to him as the Donald Manes corruption trial several years ago, as the biggest mob case he prosecuted, maybe bigger, certainly more explosive.

When he finishes, Reverend Youngblood thanks him and then says, "Mr. Mayor . . ." He describes the contexts we and most people see—the context of death itself, the context of the death of a young black man, the fact that the mayor did not attend the wake or funeral, and the mayor's reaction to the few who will always be hostile, not the vast majority looking for common sense and common decency. "Mr. Mayor . . ." Reverend Youngblood is softly preaching now. This death, like almost every death, demands restraint, silence, and respect particularly for the family of the dead. "Mr. Mayor . . ." It doesn't matter how bad or good a person the dead man may have been. Ministers bury tough and damaged people every day. And they don't read the rap sheet at the funeral. "Mr. Mayor . . ." Reverend Youngblood is quiet and steady now, teaching now. The focus should be on the family of the dead—and on the community. That's the audience. That should have been the mayor's audience, *regardless of the facts of this incident.*

On medieval maps, where the known world ended, monks would inscribe the words "Here be dragons." That's where we are now, in a place without paths, signs, or horizons, where you can't see around the next turn.

One of our team mistakenly mentions that the mayor did not attend the Diallo funeral as well.

Giuliani corrects us. "No," he says, "Howard Safir and I did attend, in the mosque in Harlem. And it was a terrible experience. We were spat on . . . and we tried to reach out to the Louima family several times."

Back and forth the conversation goes, not loud, not hostile, just quiet, direct, and tense. At one point, we ask if the mayor had read a short piece we had given him right after the Dorismond incident. Giuliani laughs. "Not only did I read it. It got me into trouble. I read it carefully and drew on some of it for a letter I wrote to Council Speaker Vallone. Unfortunately, you misspelled the Dorismond name, so I did as well. And all the papers reported that I didn't even know how to spell the name right and never commented on the content of that letter."

A little later, after the mayor mentions the incendiary statements his opponents have made, Reverend Heidi Neumark, three feet away from him, looks him in the eye and says, "You make incendiary statements too."

The temperature rises. He stares at her. "But I don't lie and I don't break federal laws and . . ." The mayor hesitates, stops himself, steers himself back to his main points.

About an hour into the discussion, Giuliani pauses, gets reflective, tells the story of this uncle's last day with the EMS. A call has come in about someone on top of the Brooklyn Bridge. For the first time in his career, his uncle doesn't want to respond, wants someone else to climb the bridge and talk the person down. But no one else takes the call, and his uncle does his job. "Maybe," says the mayor, more to himself than to us, "maybe I am the mayor of the police force, the EMS, the people I know . . . ." After one more exchange, the meeting ends. He shakes hands and rushes to leave, pressed by aides at the door to move on to his next appointment.

We remain in the meeting room and sit down to evaluate. We're tired. We have had a seventy-five-minute meeting, of an extremely sensitive nature, with a tough and determined political leader, about a topic that threatens to ignite at any moment. We feel that we have represented our people—have relayed their painful stories—as well as we possibly could. We have told him unpleasant truths. And we have listened to an intelligent, limited, flawed, ambitious power figure, not some devil, not some saint. In doing all this, we have risked all of the present and future benefits of a productive working relationship with him over this literally life-and-death matter.

These leaders, who like and respect one another, begin to savor the tension of this long and challenging morning. I tell them what they already know and feel: that they have run an unusual and extraordinary action this morning. It was an action that could not have taken place with media in the room or even outside the door, with trust in doubt or in question. It was an action that depended on the existence of an intricate and long-term public relationship—the periods of cooperation and the period of confrontation and mutual antagonism. It was an action that tested the boundaries of that relationship. And its "success" didn't depend on getting the mayor to agree to the policy points that we brought along and handed to Deputy Mayor Coles at the end. It was an action that didn't generate an immediate reaction.

What were the mayor's eventual reactions? In the days and weeks that followed, he seemed to moderate his tone and to try to identify more with the entire community. Some months later, he let it be known that two topflight public safety officials, Corrections Commissioner Bernard Kerik and First Deputy Police Commissioner Joe Dunne, were in the running to replace current NYPD head Howard Safir. Many people were surprised. We were not. The mayor chose Kerik, who went right to work to repair relations with New York's African-American and Hispanic communities and to preserve the remarkable improvements in police performance that had led to record reductions in crime. All across the board, from parks to sanitation, from housing to transportation, mayoral agencies continued to work closely and creatively with our organizations on a wide range of major initiatives.

PART III

The Habit of Organization

CHAPTER 8

The Hard Edges of
Effective Organization

In a leafy suburban town, a close friend invited me to a breakfast meeting devoted to the topic of developing the suburb's town center. After we helped ourselves to eggs and toast, coffee and juice, we sat at tables of ten, in a pleasant hotel dining room, and did the rounds. About forty people—business leaders, library and YMCA directors, university professors, neighborhood residents, and others—introduced themselves. Some people spoke briefly. Others took a great deal of time—quietly grinding an ax or two. It took nearly one hour of the proposed ninety-minute meeting just to get through the rounds.

The chairman mentioned a closed-door meeting of architects scheduled to take place in three weeks. The architects would produce several preliminary plans. But that announcement triggered a strong reaction from another friend and neighbor who argued that a more open process of house meetings, involving hundreds of residents, should occur before any closed-door sessions with professionals.

In response to this critique, the meeting veered into an extended discussion about where and when these proposed house meetings should be conducted. Lists of locations appeared on large sheets of poster paper. Someone suggested using trained facilitators for the house meetings. Another person, a little distracted and disconnected, asked about the budget for this effort. At the ninety-minute mark, I put my yellow pad away and prepared to leave. I whispered a question to a woman who represented the local library. "How long have you been talking about library expansion and these other things?" She hesitated a bit before she said, "Twenty-seven years." The chair was now talking about setting up a website (a website! I muttered to myself). And then he announced the formation of committees, including a "process" committee, which would meet soon. I headed for the nearest exit.

A few weeks later, in an inner-city parish, the pastor invited me to assist him and his lay leaders in organizing a stewardship campaign—an attempt to increase the weekly giving of people in the pews. On a Tuesday evening, I sat in a dimly lit room with the pastor and a dozen of his leaders. Several important leaders were missing. I wondered where they were. The pastor informed me that they were next door, running the parish bingo game. I then learned that the parish sponsored bingo two nights each week. Many of the most talented people in the parish called out numbers, inhaled clouds of cigarette smoke, argued with maniacal bingo players, cooked in the kitchen to keep the grouchy bingo players fed, and spent untold hours in meetings coordinating their efforts. On top of all of this, the bingo games netted very little income for the parish.

One of America's most precious social resources is the vast and deep pool of time and energy that scores of millions continue to commit to their communities, congregations, union locals, tenants councils, homeowners groups, chambers of commerce, political clubs, community boards, PTAs, sports programs, and citizens organizations. Like oil, the supply is enormous, but not unlimited. It can be polluted, wasted, or exhausted. Many voluntary organizations squander that commitment. Like American car companies in the seventies, they continue to operate in ways that succeeded for decades, when supplies of fuel seemed unending and costs remained low, but have since become obsolete. Groups have become too predictable, too slow, too inefficient, too costly, too similar to one another, and more vulnerable to competition for people's time and attention.

This trend will continue—and more Americans will choose either to bowl alone or not bowl at all—until the leaders and organizers of our voluntary associations confront a few major failings.

Leaders Don't Disorganize Enough

Very few people argue with the need for reorganizing. But they become timid, tense, or defensive when you suggest that they disorganize anything. The pastor in the inner-city parish should disorganize the bingo games that sap the energy of his best leaders and produce little or no income for the congregation. Until he does, he will not have access to the majority of his best leaders. Any attempt to run a stewardship drive that depends on the complete commitment of all of his talented people will struggle or fail. He worries about the implications of doing this, as he should. Bingo players may be irate. Bingo workers may feel that they have failed somehow. Confused parishioners, believing the bingo to be profitable, may protest. And the archdiocese, already tired of subsidizing the congregation, could interpret this as an attempt by the parish to ignore its financial obligations. The political consequences of disorganization seem much more complicated than the cost of just letting it continue. But the costs of maintaining the status quo keep increasing—and may include a failed stewardship drive.

In many congregations and organizations, thirty of the thirty-five groups are useless—with thirty sets of officers, thirty monthly meetings, thirty needs for meeting space, thirty demands for staff attention, thirty sets of minutes, and thirty additional occasions for infighting and frustration. People dutifully serve. People "plug into" slots into one or more these groups. People spend four or five nights a week out, instead of one or two. People sleep less, relax less, and create less. There may be no clear financial loss in these organizations, but there is clearly an enormous social loss to congregations, communities, and cities when large numbers of their most valuable leaders squander their time in meaningless tasks and numbing meetings.

On the other hand, the leaders who inspected the ten food stores in Brooklyn many years ago had a wonderful time. They enjoyed the preparation, the action, and the capitulation of the food storeowners. The only mistake that the leaders could have made would have been to form a permanent food store inspection committee. They were smarter than that. They scheduled a recognition event for those who had worked the hardest on the campaign, treated everyone to a night of soft drinks and pastry and informal discussion, and then disbanded the ad hoc group. The mission had been accomplished. The results were positive. It was time to turn to other matters—either in people's public or private lives. No one objected. Several of the people involved never did another thing but always remembered their participation in the inspections as a wonderful and enjoyable moment. The majority took a break and then began to ask one of the most beautiful questions in all of organizing: "What do we do next?" The answer to which was: "What do you *want* to do next?"

It takes a high level of confidence and security for leaders in voluntary organizations to disorganize failing groups and an even higher level to succeed at something, like the inspection of the stores in Brooklyn, and then let the leaders go.

One answer to the question—why do bad organizations happen to good people?—is that "good" people don't demand that their institutions disorganize more. They don't insist that they be allowed to drop doing something else, when asked to do something new. They don't see disorganizing as vital to the health and well-being of their fellow leaders, their treasured institutions, and themselves. And they don't see it as a first step toward starting or refounding new and better organizations.

People Rarely See Themselves as Founders or Refounders of Organizations

The very word—organization—seems to imply certain unquestioned qualities. Organizations have buildings and offices, physical structures and modern equipment. Organizations have committees and meetings and conferences—all of the procedural structures that we have grown used to and that universities train scores of thousands of people per year to manage or study or improve. Organizations have "old" paper—letterhead, cards, stationery, and reports. And they now have what we call "new" paper—videos, websites, and PowerPoint presentations. When pressed, people often describe their organizations by telling others where they are located, what nights of the week they meet, and where to write or e-mail to get material.

Since most of us inherit organizations that we manage, rather than starting organizations that we build, we either have a limited sense or a faded memory of what organizations looked like, felt like, and acted like when they began. We forget that labor unions used to be action organizations, that the organizers and leaders were more important than the lawyers and business agents, that the first contracts were one-page documents that the least educated worker could understand and promote and defend. Now contracts run into the hundreds of pages. Now unions need entire law firms, costing millions per year, to read and interpret them. Now the business agents and executives dominate. Now every union needs a fancy headquarters. All this while membership plummets and participation fades.

We walk into churches, synagogues, and mosques that other people built. We serve on committees set up by leaders who are long gone, who were responding to different pressures and demands. We take roles in activities originally designed to address needs that were real fifty years ago, or twenty years ago, but that have long since disappeared or changed.

We fail to appreciate the unconscious, powerful, magnetic pull of an organizational culture focused on buildings, procedures, and paper until we find ourselves sitting in a hotel dining room twenty-seven years after the first discussion of the need to expand a small suburban library, until we survey an auditorium jammed with three hundred executives and activists who work for development groups that produce almost no housing, or until we glance into the basement of a Manhattan church and see harried leaders running a noisy, unprofitable bingo game.

We can counter this magnetic pull first by recognizing its existence and its strength, then by asking the radical questions Peter Drucker posed more than a half century ago. What is our business or mission? What should it be? What will it be? And who are our customers or constituents? Who will they be? Who should they be? If we answer honestly, we will disorganize many of the organizations, committees, and groups that we now waste our time with. We will begin to think of how to start from scratch or, sometimes more practically, how to refound or restart an organization we value but which needs gut rehabilitation, not a new layer of paint.

In the Industrial Areas Foundation, we deliberately create new organizations—each with a new mix of leaders, different set of member institutions, new name, new bank account, new founding assembly, and new identity—not coalitions or alliances of existing groups. The process of founding a new organization is freeing, demanding, and exhilarating. Leaders can become equal co-owners of the new entity—a critical opportunity rarely open to us in a public arena largely crowded and dominated by established groups with well-entrenched operatives clinging to most of the lead roles. Leaders can confront the critical questions of origin and mission. Should we even be? What should we be? How should we be and what should we do? Leaders can engage in actions that are not in the least canned or stale. Leaders can learn to plan, act, experiment, fail, evaluate, act again, and succeed. They can experience directly the joys and sorrows of creating an organization that may have the power to shape communities and cities, to improve whole regions, and to influence, someday, a nation. By doing so, they can become refounding brothers and sisters of their country and can write the next and newest chapters in American social and political history.

CHAPTER 9

Disorganizing and Reorganizing

In 1979, Ed Chambers asked me if my wife and I would consider moving to Baltimore. The IAF had started a new organization there about four years before, and it was already in trouble. If we had known how much trouble, we may not have packed our belongings and our dog into our Chevy Nova and headed east. When we arrived, on the weekend of the Three Mile Island meltdown, after barely surviving an avalanche of boulders on the Pennsylvania Turnpike, we learned the total and terrible truth.

Our relatively new power organization had already imploded. Instead of a solid budget and a sound dues base, it was twenty thousand dollars in debt and dropping fast. Instead of forty or fifty member congregations, there were five or six, and disputes threatened to reduce that number even further. It had several paid staff—none of whom were up to the job and all of whom needed to be fired. The first ministers' meeting I attended drew a total of four pastors—two of whom could not contain their intense dislike for one another. And, in the first action that I observed, on my third day in the city, the two leaders running the action disagreed publicly with one another—one leader pressing the agenda of the organization, the other leader siding with the mayor when the mayor said that he couldn't do much about the plague of rats overrunning certain communities. I went home that night and told my wife that we should unpack slowly.

The temptation (other than to flee) would have been to try to find some large issue, or dramatic cause, to rally the group around. Instead, we began a long and difficult process of disorganizing and reorganizing this wreck of an organization. Week after week, month after month, I worked with a small team of determined leaders to raise money, to pay down the debt, and to recruit new dues-paying congregations. We pushed out one of the incompetent staff people and several of the undisciplined and negative leaders. Slowly and incrementally, with many setbacks, we sought to rebuild trust and confidence among the top leaders. At the end of this phase, the organization, still shaky, still in debt, still in doubt, was able to hold a public assembly of one thousand leaders, from twenty institutions, who were at least clear that they needed to continue to address the basics—dues, fundraising, recruitment, and leadership training—if they were ever to have real power in Baltimore.

At the end of fifteen months, for a variety of reasons, I gladly moved on to New York to begin the EBC organization, and Arnie Graf moved to Baltimore to pick up and accelerate the difficult work of disorganizing and reorganizing BUILD. Arnie is as persistent, focused, and creative an organizer as you will ever meet, but the challenge in Baltimore absorbed every ounce of determination, patience, and imagination that he could muster.

At least four more years of steady work followed, with Gerald Taylor assisting Arnie during part of this phase. Finally, mostly due to Arnie and Gerald's efforts and the extraordinary commitment of leaders like Phyllis Douglass and Marion Dixon, Msgr.

Claire O'Dwyer and the incomparable Reverend Vernon Dobson, BUILD reemerged, nearly eight years after its bumpy beginning, as the premier power organization in the city. By then, it was nearly a new organization—many new leaders, topflight new staff, money in the bank, new institutional members, and a new agenda of issues and actions that demanded the attention of the Baltimore establishment. It went on to author the country's first successful living wage legislation. It imagined and created an authority to fund after school programs—the BUILD Child First Authority—again the first of its kind in an American city. It rebuilt forgotten corners of a forgotten city with handsome, new Nehemiah homes. It conceived of the nation's first Joseph Plan—a state strategy to set aside surplus funds during boom years to bolster threatened social spending during leaner times—and now helps implement it. It became one of the most important citizens power organization in the region and is now one of the three or four most effective power groups in the nation.

In the early eighties, a parish in the Bushwick section of Brooklyn joined East Brooklyn Congregations. Its dwindling congregation of 150 members met in a crumbling cavern of a church building in a community that had suffered years of white flight and arson. The building needed hundreds of thousands of dollars in repairs. And the diocese was threatening to shut the doors. When I asked the four staff members—Fr. Ed Brady, Sr. Frances Gritte, Fr. Lew Maynard, and Sr. Maryellen Kane—why they had decided to join the organization, they answered honestly: they felt that they had absolutely nothing to lose and wondered whether they could try to apply the universals of the IAF approach in a last-ditch attempt to disorganize and reorganize the parish.

We met for days, a few miles from the smoldering streets of Bushwick, in the peaceful backyard of Sr. Frances's home in nearby Queens, where an occasional bird twittered at us from up in the trees. I provided training on how to do individual meetings, on the tension between a relational culture and the typical bureaucratic culture we find in most congregations, and on the identification and engagement of talented new leaders. They argued and struggled among themselves as to how they would relate to one another. They wondered how they would fend off resistance to any new approach from the parish's small but fierce old guard. And they schemed to find ways to finesse the diocese while quietly pursuing this organizational experiment.

At the end of several months of training and strategy, the staff came to a critical decision: everything that they did—beyond liturgy and necessary crisis response—would be put to a simple test. Did the activity lead to the training and developing of leaders? Or not? If it did, they would invest their time and energy in it. If it did not, they would avoid it, or withdraw from it.

If you have ever run a parish, business, or agency, you know how radical this decision was. For the parish staff, it meant saying no to the existing groups and cliques that had come to expect a member of the parish staff to sit through three-hour meetings of unbearable boredom. In dying parishes, this practice is rationalized as a "ministry of presence."

The staff encouraged veteran leaders to think differently, and individual staff members mentored, supported, and trained key leaders who were open to change. But when entrenched leaders refused to respond, then the staff moved ahead and sought out newer, more open, less "established" leaders with vision, energy, and a following.

The staff stopped being managers, paper-pushers, baby-sitters, or reactors. They became talent scouts, coaches, teachers, and trainers. They also moved aggressively beyond the walls of the existing parish and sought out the majority of members not yet in the pews. They went into the Hope Gardens housing projects, into the tenements along Central Avenue, into welfare offices, and into public schools. The pastor even visited one of the low-wage knitting mills that employed many of his monolingual, Spanish-speaking members. I walked in with him one morning. The workers were bent over tables overflowing with fabric, intent on their sewing and in fear of the owner. We had heard how he enforced discipline: by brandishing a bolo knife now and then. When the first worker spotted Fr. Brady, her face went from stunned surprise to joy to gratitude, while the expression of the owner, eying us through the glass wall of his office, hardened.

Slowly, after hundreds of individual meetings and scores of house meetings and block meetings, after a phase of direct action on matters of immediate concern, the congregation began to grow. Sunday attendance went from 150 to 400 after about six months of work. Then, six months later, 800 began to worship. Then 1,000. Then, after two years, nearly 1,500 people refilled the large, ornate, crumbling Catholic church. The diocese responded by committing to fund the renovation of the church building. Artisans repaired the roof, patched holes, and repainted the gold leaf in the vault over the altar.

The pastor, largely unrecognized for his remarkable work, was quietly transferred. One by one, the other staff members moved on. A determined and experienced new duo, Msgr. John Powis and Sr. Kathy Maire, took over and kept pushing the parish forward. St. Barbara's is now vital, teeming, complicated, and challenging—central to a community hungry for a stable institution that can effectively anchor neighborhood life.

As the Nehemiah Homes were being built, the EBC staff of three—Stephen Roberson, Lucille Clark, and I—worked in a third floor office housed in a ramshackle rectory off Eastern Parkway and Rockaway Avenue in Brooklyn. To reach us, visitors needed to walk through the line of men waiting to eat in the soup kitchen on the first floor, to slide through another line of people outside a social service office on the second floor, and then to climb a narrow set of stairs to the third floor. The offices themselves were decent, but spare. Burglar gates covered the windows.

One morning, we received a visit from the commissioner of community development from Nassau County, Long Island. He was a very dapper fellow, indeed. He wore a handsomely tailored suit, carried an expensive attaché case, and sported all of the most up-do-date insignia worn by the successful executive corps. He had read about our strategy to build thousands of new single-family homes and wanted to meet with us to find out how we were going about it.

As we shook hands, before we sat down, he made an announcement. "I'm sorry to say this, but I can tell you right now that you can't possibly succeed."

Stephen and I stared at him for a moment. Then I said, "Well, you could save us a hell of a lot of time and trouble by telling us how you know that."

The executive looked around the office, at the furniture, the worn wooden floors, the gates on the windows, and said, "This place lacks the proper ambience for success . . ."

Ambience. Stephen and I repeated the word to one another for a few moments.

The executive hadn't asked a single question about who we were, who we had hired to help build the homes, how we had raised millions of dollars of no interest construction financing, what we saw as our fundamental mission, or what actions we had already taken or were planning to take. No, he focused on the outward signs of "organization"—buildings, equipment, structures, paper, image, ambience—and jumped to his stunning conclusion.

(By the way, several years later, we read that our visitor committed crimes while in office, was indicted, and spent several years in prison.)

Effective organization doesn't begin with furniture, office complexes, and snazzy logos. It begins with a team of talented leaders, clear on its mission, and willing to act to try to accomplish that mission. Great companies start this way. Great religious congregations, denominations, faiths originate this way. And a living democracy and vital society start and restart here.

You won't find examples of this living and breathing democracy in well-appointed offices or in expensive hotel conference centers. You won't find them in the creaking chairs and roped-off pews set aside for "community input" by the managers of the political establishment. You'll find them at unexpected times and in unusual places—like on a sultry night not long ago in lower Manhattan.

The corner of Pitt and Stanton, near where Houston meets the East River, shimmers in the evening sun. There's too little space, too little air, too little elbowroom. It's a neighborhood that seems to have tumbled out of one of Richard Scarry's "world's busiest" children's books, with planes, boats, trains, cars, and characters packed into every corner of every page.

I've arrived early, so I take a walk around the neighborhood—past a small synagogue graced by a beautiful flower garden, past a New Age restaurant serving sandwiches with sprouts and lots of bottled water, past a youth center humming with shouts and cries, kids spilling out the door and onto the sidewalk and street. Our Lady of Sorrows Church and School and Rectory appear jammed, like an afterthought, into an already crowded row of tenements. The church buildings seem hunched, squeezed.

Across the street, three large trailers are parked. These trailers serve as the mobile headquarters for a movie in production. Danny Glover stars, I'm told. The shooting takes place at 3:00 A.M. In front of the church, the movie's food service is set up—serving chicken, fruit, and drinks to workers, street people, passersby, and extras. But who is who? I can't sort out the characters from the "characters," and neither can the canteen crew, who happily serve food to whoever stops by.

Downstairs in the church hall, the meeting room begins to fill—as if the fullness of the street is seeping into every available space. The church basement is divided in two by a partition. On one side of the partition, about 150 leaders of Lower Manhattan Together will meet. On the other side, the extras for the movie will muster. A few of the LMT leaders wander into the extras portion of the hall. Several extras mistake our group for the movie company.

At half past seven, starting time, the room is packed. Angel Diaz chairs tonight's meeting. But "chair" is the wrong word. He doesn't have a chair tonight—just a microphone and a spot, front and center, and complete command of himself and his surroundings. When he asks the group to stand for the opening prayer, the group rises. And Reverend Vanderjaat, the pastor of Middle Collegiate Church, prays.

Reverend Vanderjaat has a reddish beard, long face, and the body of a distance runner. The prayer he leads is heard by a diverse group—Anglo Saxons like Hubble-Riggs and Warnick, ethnic Catholics like Connelly and Gurdack, Hispanics like Nieves and Hidalgo and Gonzalez, African Americans from a struggling Presbyterian church at 6th and the FDR Drive, a Jewish foundation director, a daughter of a sitting Supreme Court Justice, and a Chinese not-for-profit executive.

If all God's children aren't here tonight, *most* of them are represented, heads bowed in prayer above the low murmur of the movie extras. Scanning the crowd is like looking at an exposed side of a mountain. There, in the rock face, the layers of sediment tell the story of the earth—a geological petition with the signatures of many millennia.

Tonight, you see the human layers that make up this city—the

Dutch and the English, the Jews and Italians, the Greeks and African Americans, the Hispanics and Asians. One after another, they have come. They have settled in and settled down, one group on top of another, layer upon layer.

For ninety minutes, tonight, they will operate together, mix with one another, become greater than the sum of the parts of their diverse and distinct identities, but not so expansive and diluted as to drift into some photo-op of an idealized American "family." In action, they represent a something-in-between-the-local-and-the-national, a mediating group, a kind of informal congress, that functions in ways and produces results that no local group or national body can achieve.

When the prayer ends, Mr. Diaz takes charge. He is five foot six inches tall, dressed in a white shirt and tie, pleasant and upbeat, confident and in control. He reviews the business of the night—celebrating major improvements in pedestrian safety along Houston Street, announcing a new campaign to conduct citizen inspections of public housing projects, and continuing to press forward on significant park improvements in lower Manhattan. Mr. Diaz is a manager of public housing by day, leader in his congregation and LMT by night. He is moderate, thorough, balanced, and persistent.

Mr. Diaz calls on a leader from First Presbyterian Church, Liz Hubbell-Riggs, to review the progress made on pedestrian safety and to deal with the City's Department of Transportation Manhattan commissioner, who is attending tonight's session. The lights switch off, and Ms. Hubbell-Riggs leads the group through a before-and-after slide show of dangerous intersections that have been improved because of LMT's efforts. After each of a dozen improvements, Ms. Hubbell-Riggs praises the city official and thanks him. The rhythm of her presentation—the dangers before, upgrades after, and thanks—engages the crowd. The commissioner is pleased. He's beginning to beam. When it is his turn to respond, he says that he felt that he was "home," in the parish he attended thirty-eight years before, in the school he was graduated from, among people from another parish where he had served as an altar boy. The group applauds him.

At the end of the litany, another leader, a young Episcopal priest named Jeremy Warnick, steps to the microphone and brings up another dangerous intersection—Houston and the FDR Drive —that has not yet been addressed. The commissioner becomes subdued, more formal. His voice takes on the tone of a city bureaucrat who is not at all at home. He says he will need to "take that request under advisement." Fr. Warnick presses and asks for a response in the near future. The commissioner responds positively but is clearly less comfortable than when he was regaling the group about his altar boy days.

The entire exchange is a good example of how we try to conduct public business—giving ample credit where it is due, but not sliding into false familiarity or hero-worship. Our leaders remind the official that there is more work to be done. They inject a necessary edge into the encounter. The commissioner walks out of the room and hesitates in the hallway. He has been applauded, recognized, challenged, and warned—all in just a few well-paced minutes. He feels basically positive, but decidedly mixed, which is fine with the leaders who thank him for his time and remind him that they will be calling.

The next part of the meeting focuses on the inspections of four large housing projects conducted by LMT leaders and staff. Again, the lights go down and the leaders narrate the conditions contained in the slides that appear on the screen. When the slides show large rat holes and overflowing garbage bins, the crowd quietly groans. The leaders have created LMT report cards for each project, and the first grades given are not high—mostly C's and

D's. Reverend Getty Cruz conducts this part of the meeting and proposes that the group take these grades to the project managers, not the media, to see if they will respond. If they don't improve, then the group would make the evaluations public. There is unanimous support for this tactic, and the attention of the leaders shifts to parks.

LMT has pressed for and secured major commitments to Seward Park and East River Park. The mayor announced the renovation of East River Park in his January State of the City address. A Parks Department senior architect, George Vellonakis, is there to present his renderings of the park improvements. He shows where new walkways, play areas, and benches will be placed. Five million dollars will begin the reclaiming of this worn public space. Then Fr. Joseph Gurdak, dressed in the brown robes of his Franciscan order, reminds the leaders that this young architect also produced the design for the newly renovated City Hall Park. Robust applause follows—and continues for more than a minute. Mr. Vellonakis seems to relish this moment. The people of the city are giving him as warm and as generous an evaluation as he may ever receive in his public life.

The meeting ends at 9:01, a minute late. But even though the heat and humidity have taken their toll, people don't bolt from their chairs and rush out into the night. People are damp, but not tired. Many stay and chat, gathering spontaneously in groups of four or five all around the hall. That's the first, informal evaluation of the work of the night.

At least twenty leaders remain for the second, more formal evaluation that the lead organizer, Joe Morris, has asked me to conduct. We review several of the key factors that made the night a success—the intense preparation that Joe has demanded of his leaders, the nearly flawless coordination of verbal presentation and visual aids, the tension injected artfully at the end of the transportation commissioner's appearance, and the tone created by Angel Diaz's apparently easy mastery of the pace of the event. We focus for a few moments on how to make sure the newer leaders feel more comfortable in their roles.

At twenty past nine, I wrap up the evaluation and ask people how they feel. Everyone is positive. One man puts it best, "I feel so much better than when I walked in tonight, energized, enthusiastic . . ."

And that's how I feel, as I hail a cab on Houston Street and race through this beautiful, balmy New York night.

PART IV

The Habit of Reflection

CHAPTER 10

Three Public Cultures

Nearly thirty years ago, those of us who organized saw our work as primarily political. We operated with local leaders and local institutions, and we engaged the powerful leaders and institutions of the public and private sectors. We were from, in, and of neighborhoods and communities, ethnic and racial groups. We were *not* downtown. We were *not* City Hall. In fact, we were "political" in the original, seventeenth-century definition of the term, described by Bernard Crick in his excellent book, *In Defence of Politics:* we defined ourselves as antiestablishment. In the 1970s in Chicago, we were not doing battle with the crown, the king, and the cardinal, but their modern descendants—a dominant mayor and his corrupt court, real estate predators, racist school superintendents, tyrannical factory owners, mafia bandits, and the haughty heads of major banks and savings and loans. Our challenge was to leverage one part of the public sector against another, the federal government against segregated states; or one part of the private sector against another, publicity conscious banks against sleazy mortgage bankers; or one part of the public sector against an out-of-control market, a national community reinvestment act against savings and loans unwilling to lend in local communities. We hadn't yet developed the ego or the insight to stake out and re-inforce a third, essential sector that was as consistently *for* as it was persistently *against*.

Today, to organize effectively and participate with impact, it's important to see the activity of organizing as something even more central and fundamental and radical—cultural work. When you focus on culture, or cultures, you take into account habits, pat-terns, beliefs, symbols, heroes and heroines, including your own, not just legislation and policies, elections and appointments, cur-rent causes or party platforms. Cultures move like great plates, often unheard and unseen, below the surface, shaping and trans-forming the terrain we operate on. When these plates collide, when cultures occasionally clash, the impact can be violent and profound.

I am going to describe the interplay of three cultures—a mar-ket culture that thrives in the private sector for the most part, a bu-reaucratic culture that finds its most accommodating home in the public sector, and a relational culture that should, and sometimes does, reside in the third or voluntary sector. While each culture suits a particular sector, in reality aspects of all three cultures oper-ate *within* each sector, as well. Some businesses, for example, can be terribly bureaucratic, while others understand the value of rela-tionships. Some government services can be delivered with the same aggressiveness and concern for quality that the market gener-ates. And some voluntary organizations tie themselves in orga-nizational knots, reading *Robert's Rules of Order* and generating endless committees and task forces, rather than focusing on their mission and engaging others in it.

But the exceptions to the general rule do not disprove it; they just complicate it. Each culture produces, transmits, and promotes a set of basic values. Understanding the nature of each culture—each cluster of values and beliefs—is critical. And remaining alert to the tensions and strains among them is essential to modern citizens willing both to explore and to shape the new American landscape.

The Market Culture

Someday, we will reach that moment in our history when an American can write both positively and critically about the market culture and not be stereotyped as a closet socialist. I hope, by now, you'll believe me when I say that I am a credit-card-carrying consumer who occasionally goes to the mall. I admire the market's energy, appreciate its power, and am concerned about its impact. I acknowledge its place in our lives, but, like most Americans, I don't worship it. And I've spent a significant part of my life working with people to keep it in its place.

The market culture, for all of its emphasis on personal initiative and individual choice, is composed at its core of institutions. Financial institutions, information and technology companies, old manufacturers and new manufacturers—institutions large and small start, grow, collide, compete, collapse, merge, and regroup. The rate of change within and among some of these institutions is often remarkable—far greater than the pace in the other two cultures. Thirty years ago, the number of computer workers was in the low hundreds of thousands in a handful of companies. Today, more than two million Americans work in the computer field. It's as if a new charismatic religious movement emerged and swept across the country in little more than three decades. Thirty years ago, my mother and father walked to work—my mother to her office job in the TootsieToy Company, my father to his security job at Newark Electronics, both on Pulaski Road. Today, a South

Asian group, described in a recent *Harvard Business Review* article, custom-builds factories and hires a local work force to produce clothing in response to a specific order from a specific company. When the large order is filled, the group often dismantles the factory and sets up shop in another, cheaper country to fill a future order. This group opens and closes facilities almost as if they were parts of a stock portfolio that can be bought and sold with ease. Suspend judgment for a moment on the damage to the environment, the impact on the lives of the temporarily employed workers, and the pressure this puts on third-world nations to provide tax breaks and other inducements. Take the time to appreciate the focus, the speed, and the adaptability of those on the edgy margins of the market culture.

The most successful institutions in the market culture invest in themselves. The more bureaucratic institutions of the public sector and more relational voluntary institutions of the third sector spend almost nothing. The best market institutions change systematically and budget billions for new talent and new technologies. Microsoft alone spends more than two billion for research and development. This sector understands institutional mortality— struggle, attacks, counterattacks, and casualties—more than the others. Its theorists boast about the "creative destruction" that occurs in the business world. In fact, everything that the market does, including its occasional catastrophic and costly failures, is considered "good."

One passenger on an Acela train tearing through the ruins of North Philadelphia might be saddened by what he or she sees. Where did all the workers and families go? What will become of the emptied churches, sagging homes, and crumbling schools? Where's the return on the investment of billions in public dollars poured religiously into tourism, hotels, and sports arenas and all the other quasi-market remedies to urban decay? A companion with a market perspective might see the natural order of things, might picture all the new enterprises in the corporate campuses of Valley Forge, Pennsylvania, that have replaced these dying industries, might take clients and friends to the opera or an Eagles game, might consider the public money spent on games and arts for her and her peers a far better investment than increased funding for affordable housing for the invisible women and men who work in the hotel kitchens, or clean the new stadium, or guard the arts center door.

The market culture has a clear and powerful dynamic running through its center, like a unifying theme: the dynamic of buying and selling, trading and exchanging, moving money and moving goods. This dynamic defines the major roles within this culture—the roles of innovator, producer, seller, marketer, and consumer. The culture turns almost everything into a commodity—time, water, pleasure, and ideas; home mortgages, neighborhoods, downtowns, and entire cities; what used to be considered *social* security, honors like the Heisman Trophy, disasters like September 11, and even the heroism displayed that day. And when it runs short of actual commodities, it invents "futures" of the commodities, and then trades "options" on futures of commodities. It's a clear and focused culture, with a potent internal drive that tries to carry everyone and everything with it toward a bottom line of profit or of loss.

Those within the market culture willingly bear witness to their values. They fervently believe that the freest market is the best market. Society is best served when each isolated individual has the opportunity to make independent and free decisions in his or her own interest—billions and billions of such decisions. In fact, as the political philosopher William Sullivan has written, the market promotes the notion of the "non-reality of other institutions." People would be richer, the economy would be better, the nation would be healthier, if congregations and unions and trade groups, if environmental agencies and the IAF and the occasional inquisitive reporter, simply left well enough alone or ceased to exist. The mighty institutions of the market don't want other institutions mediating between them and their customers. The right relationship, between the market and the individual, however imbalanced it may be, *is* everything. This belief system is deep, personal, and even codified in law. The corporation is not an institution, but a "legal person." American Express, meet Mr. Cuevas.

The market culture has a new generation of heroes and heroines. Bill Gates. Ted Turner. Martha Stewart. Donald Trump. Sandy Weill. Tina Brown. The list goes on. The market is so dominant at the turn of the millennium that market heroes readily think of themselves—or are promoted by others—as potential mayors or governors, senators or presidents. Quirky old Ross Perot did remarkably well, from a standing start, with almost no political experience, in 1996. Donald Trump coyly flirted with the Reform Party in the year 2000 go-round. John Corzine went shopping in New Jersey and bought himself a seat in the United States Senate. Mike Bloomberg jumped from Wall Street to City Hall in one rather quick and costly $70 million leap.

For the most part, this new generation of computer and real estate, Internet and telecommunications billionaires is every bit as eccentric and extravagant as the characters of the last Gilded Age. But they seem somehow cleaner and smoother than automakers or railroad barons or mine owners. Soot and smoke, grease and oil, are long gone. A photograph of my grandfather, taken in the thirties, all five foot six and three hundred pounds of him, shows him sitting with his crew outside the Chicago and Northwestern Railroad yard where he worked the bellows and repaired rails. It records a world far removed from the swells who fill the Yankee Stadium boxes on a World Series night. All wealth is still welcome, but wealth without works, without sweat, without dirt, without "workers" in the old- fashioned sense, is most admired.

A vast network of secondary institutions supports the market culture. Business schools, graduate departments, and research centers send wave after wave of new and well-trained recruits to this culture. The media, now wholly owned by major corporations, give intense and favorable coverage to the leading actors and daily events of this culture. Those who market books—not the producing authors, the publishers, or the consuming readers—often determine which books make it and which do not. This sprawling and confident culture keeps creating new wealth, new myths, new foundations, new supplicants, new casualties, and new dependents.

The market culture has phenomenal range and reach. It operates twenty-four hours per day, seven days a week. In the not-so-distant past, there used to be a central commercial district, business hours, blue laws, days and places that were off limits to the market. Today, through television, computers and the Internet, the market penetrates all time and space. Worldwide trading is continuous. The appeal to people's needs and wants, along with the manufacturing of new needs and wants, is incessant—as incessant as the ability of the market to respond to those who decide to shop and buy.

With both political parties and most American opinion leaders and shapers either directly or indirectly in the employ of the market—a kind of one-party domination and private sector patronage binge that would have earned the admiration of the coldest and crustiest ward heeler in the old Cook County Democratic machine—it is not surprising that there is so little sustained discussion or debate about the limits of the market and the damage it can do.

The Bureaucratic Culture

Now, don't get me wrong. In criticizing the market, I'm not necessarily arguing on behalf of the barnacles stuck to the hull of the bureaucratic culture. This culture tends to thrive in school systems, penal systems, public health agencies, housing authorities, municipal and federal agencies, some parts of large corporations, and, increasingly, large not-for-profit organizations. We have all gnashed our teeth while waiting on line in the state's Department of Motor Vehicles. We suffer regularly in the lower and middle rungs of vast public agencies. Recently, a tenant leader in a Bronx housing development called the maintenance office four times over a two-hour period, as water gushed into her unit from the apartment above. Utterly frustrated, her apartment destroyed, she called the police and threatened to kill the superintendent if they didn't come. They arrived immediately, rushed into her flooded flat, and, seeing the situation, helped her get a maintenance crew to respond. Bureaucratic culture is fractal, repeating itself across all scales of an organization and permeating even the smallest institutions. A tenants' council of five members, or a church committee of eight, can be as rule-bound, by-the-book, and spiritually listless as the spectacularly inept New York City Board of Education.

The main dynamic and reason for being of the bureaucratic culture is to provide service. That dynamic generates its own set of roles—manager, service provider, consultant, client. A rhythm of meetings, planning, memos, reports, studies, and more meetings ripples through this culture. One example: several years ago, the head of the New York State Bankers Association at the time, a leader of East Brooklyn Congregations, and I had scheduled a meeting with the Board of Education to discuss EBC's attempt to link high school graduates to bank jobs and private college scholarships. The three of us sat in the Bankers Association conference room and watched, in disbelief, as twenty-three Board of Education managers filed in the door and filled every seat in the room. This show of middle manager muscle wasn't to embrace and advance our initiative, but to ensnare it in red tape and slow it down and, if possible, kill it. Principals asked us *not* to offer these opportunities, "so that the children won't be disappointed." Administrators failed to open libraries for the private college recruiters eager to interview students. One principal lowered her voice and said, "You don't understand, do you? This is not a school. It's a social service center."

The core belief system of much of the modern bureaucratic culture is that the world—particularly the world of the poor and the marginalized—is a universe of *needs*, not of persons, of *disabilities*, not capacities. The rational approach is to identify each need and to design a program to meets that need, regularly and repetitively, often for large numbers of people. Managers, service providers, and evaluators are required to manage and implement and measure the outcomes of every program targeted to every need.

The goal of efficiently delivering services that meet needs led experts in New York in the late sixties to transform the way social workers operated. Until then, each social worker dealt with a limited number of families on a wide range of issues—housing assistance, job training, health care, welfare payments, and so on. Their fundamental focus was on the family. Then officials in the public sector and progressive politicians fell under the spell of private sector efficiency experts. Some workers initially preferred to remain safe and secure in a central office, rather than out on the streets of the city. Some recipients of public assistance resented the sometimes patronizing, sometimes racist attitudes of some social workers. Public sector unions, themselves mostly managed by bureaucrats, traded old-fashioned professionalism and impact for "modern" quality control and predictability.

In the reorganized workplace, each worker began to specialize in one aspect of one program of the social welfare system, mimicking the private sector's assembly-line system. The worker saw hundreds of clients, or reviewed hundreds of forms, to respond to one crisis or address one immediate need. Social workers no longer had time to know the people they dealt with, along with their families and communities. Regular home visits stopped. Anonymity became the norm. And dissatisfaction among the best social workers—no longer able to see any impact of their work in human terms—deepened.

This reform failed utterly to meet the needs of the poor but succeeded beyond anyone's expectations at feeding the growing appetite of the management class. Like those in the market culture, these professionals either believed in, or wished for, the nonreality of other institutions—family, congregation, and community. There was no room or appreciation for the often-unmeasurable impact of meaningful public relationships, for spirit, for affinity, or for soul. And, in the most negative and cynical corners of this culture, there was contempt for family, community, and organized religion of all kinds.

The crude corruption and grotesque expansion of the American welfare system throughout the seventies and eighties were followed by the crude reduction and grotesque "reform" of the welfare system in the late nineties. Both were made possible by the triumphant hijacking of American social services by the bureaucratic culture in the sixties. In fact, wherever the bureaucratic culture became synonymous with the public sector the quality of service declined, the tendency of the bureaucracy to turn inward and satisfy its own needs increased, and the scorn of those who had contempt for "big government" resonated more with a frustrated and alienated public.

Of course, there *are* needs in our society—a need for security in our cities and suburbs, a need for quality education for scores of millions of school children, a need for adequate public housing for 750,000 people in just one city, New York, who cannot come close to paying what the market insists is a fair rate for shelter. And these needs demand large-scale, well-organized, far-ranging institutions to meet them. One such agency, the Works Progress Administration, added untold billions in new public works to the nation during the Great Depression, while giving millions of idle Americans meaningful work. Another institution, the American military establishment, fought and won a world-wide war against fascism of unprecedented scale and difficulty. Closer to home, a third institution, the City of Chicago, managed to repair and expand hundreds of its formerly dreary and dangerous public school facilities. A fourth, the New York City Police Department, reversed decades of defeatism and finger-pointing with a tightly organized, computer-aided approach to fighting crime.

But the cops who led this effort—commissioners Bratton, Safir, and Kerik, deputies Timoney, Esposito, and Dunne—are the exceptions. The more common heroes and heroines of the modern bureaucratic culture are imperial executive directors and remote senior managers and, increasingly, high cost consultants. "Success" is measured by the worker's ability to get off the line, into supervision, into management. "Access" to the top of the bureaucratic heap is considered the coin of the realm. This culture often transforms successful teachers, effective cops, compelling ministers, brilliant nurses, and savvy social workers into supervisors, directors, assistant commissioners, and denominational executives. Perks, incentives, pay raises—all increase as the professional moves further and further away from contact with real people.

Like the market culture, the bureaucratic culture has a huge support system and a compelling internal logic. Professional schools charge princely sums to mint more managers and analysts.

Teachers colleges, police academies, social work schools, nursing schools, and seminaries provide training in the technical and administrative aspects of their fields but not in critical relational arts and skills. As a result, those who used to see education, social work, or police work as vocations—as honorable and laudable professions—increasingly avoid the rote curricula and peeling paint of the public school or inner-city police precinct for a cubicle in an investment firm or a private security company.

The market can be quick and hard-hitting, harsh and aggressive. The bureaucratic culture too often prides itself on being none of the above. As a rule, it's neither flexible nor nimble. It tends to be fixed in place and limited in time. It expects its clients—the young, the sick, the victim of domestic violence, the congregants, the students, the union members—to come to it, on its terms, at the hours it chooses to operate. It builds a building. It opens a center. It hires staff. It meets for hours about such matters as which cute logo or eye-catching sign or website design to select. It quickly curls inward, preoccupied with itself, loyal to itself, protecting itself—drifting further and further away from mission, from action, from relating to the people it was originally created to "serve."

The Relational Culture

But what is this third culture—the one we call "relational?" Unlike the other two cultures, whose existence and impact most would grant, both the reality of the relational culture and the fact that it has earned the right to be classed with the other two need to be asserted as well as described.

The basic member institution of the relational culture is the voluntary association—congregations, social clubs, athletic leagues, citizens organizations, parents and tenants and immigrant and homeowner groups. Ironically, many of the institutions of the current bureaucratic and market cultures started here. Most religious denominations and orders of men or women religious were begun by a few dedicated leaders, often reacting to obstacles in the more established church or diocese. The Cook County Democratic Party emerged from Scandanavian and German taverns in Chicago. Even insurance companies and savings and loan associations grew out of the early, relational gathering of congregants in the basements of their black churches, ethnic congregations, and synagogues. The associations that formed the base of the relational culture didn't depend on advice from Ivy League Ph.D.s or high-powered consultants from Arthur Anderson. They saw an abuse or an opportunity or a need. They discussed it among those they knew and trusted. They developed a response. And they went into action.

The dynamic of the relational culture is created by leaders who initiate and deepen and multiply effective public relationships. These leaders know, consciously or unconsciously, that their ability to act depends on the number and quality of relationships that they and their colleagues can muster and sustain. They see themselves as recruiters, talent scouts, and trainers. They look for other *leaders*, not passive followers or adoring dependents. Their bottom line is not profit and loss, or clients served, but expanding pools of reciprocity and trust among people who can act with purpose and power.

When they act, *as* they act, people *change*. The poor become less poor. The disconnected of all races and classes engage. The marginalized begin to move toward the center. The powerless gather, organize, and act. Victims get their first taste of victory. At the core of the relational culture is a belief in the ability of most people to grow and develop, as well as a faith in the newly arrived or recently organized people or formerly excluded people to exert their newfound power in effective and responsible ways.

The change that occurs is not entirely rational or measurable.

What motivates a teenager in a housing project in Brooklyn to take the time and run the real risks to sign up twenty-five others to participate in a church worship service? What moves a fireman to enter a building that is blazing and collapsing above him? What sustains an awkward and doubt-filled legislator as he makes his lonely, rural rounds? Whatever it is, whether specifically religious or more broadly spiritual, has little in common with the soft and fuzzy sentiments you may hear in progressive congregations or liberal political luncheons. People capable of change and committed to change emerge from a disciplined culture of individual meetings and faithful relationships, of strict training and ongoing education, and of experimental action and tough evaluation. They are steeled to survive counterattacks from both the market and the state and secure enough to seek out the best and the brightest from the other sectors when common ground can be found.

We don't yet have the language to convey what occurs at the core of a thriving relational culture. And there is no step-by-step user guide or jazzy PowerPoint presentation that can ever distill it. It is not essentially instrumental or technical, although it respects the need for knowledge and expertise. Like any other craft, it depends on high standards, experienced masters, a process of apprenticeship, and a commitment to lifelong learning and improvement. It demands of its practitioners a basic respect for the tools and the materials of the trade—in this case, the lives and spirits of fellow citizens, students, patients, tenants, and others. It is profoundly reciprocal: leader and follower, cop and citizen, social worker and tenant, nurse and patient, organizer and leader need one another for long-term success and satisfaction. And it is authoritative— embodying tested traditions, reflecting the wisdom of those who have perfected the craft—when performed professionally by the leader negotiating with a mayor, by the cop on the beat on a tough city block, by the home health attendant, or the manager of a housing project.

The key people in this culture generally don't attract the attention of Oprah, Geraldo, or Larry King Live. Their work doesn't lend itself to dramatic TV or saucy sound bites. In fact, this intricate craft cannot proceed under the glare of television lights or the impatient demands of reporters on deadline. Even the best of writers, like Samuel G. Freedman, needs three hundred pages to detail the relational work of a single schoolteacher or single Baptist minister.

The noncelebrity heroes and heroines of this culture are the Croatian pastors of the parish my father first attended in Chicago; the two women religious and two priests who brought a dying Brooklyn parish back to life; Arnie Graf and Gerald Taylor, Marion Dixon and Reverend Vernon Dobson, who willed BUILD into its present successful existence; Alice McCollum and John Heinemeier; Bishop Francis J. Mugavero and Andy Sarabia. Parents and ministers, rabbis and teachers, nurses and leaders, coaches and mentors—those in the relational culture must make subtle and complex judgments about their own capacity and the capacity of others to grow and change, in many shifting circumstances, over many years. Their judgments affect the futures of individuals, families, congregations, communities, and cities. Perhaps, when taken together, across a vast and diverse landscape, they affect the future of a nation.

And yet there is almost no organized support system, training ground, or incentive package for people who want to remain relational workers or build power in the third sector. They are rarely recognized, much less honored. Either they are patronized for doing nice, worthy, local work. Or they are promoted up into the administrative ladder—away from the very relationships that are the medium for their success and satisfaction.

In its range and reach, the relational culture can be as flexible, nimble, and aggressive as the market. You can relate and train, plan and act, almost anywhere. You can create a school without walls that embodies and teaches the values and skills of the relational culture in a church basement on the lower east side, in a Roy Rogers restaurant in downtown Baltimore, in a public school classroom in Fort Worth, Austin, or San Antonio, in a mosque on the north side of Chicago. You can simply set up shop and do your relational work wherever and whenever you have the energy and chutzpah to do it. And, when you do, you can make your own unsolicited contribution to the gross social product of the nation—more engaged and healthy citizens, more self-sufficient and able families, more decent and stable communities—in ways that neither the market can privatize nor the bureaucratic culture co-opt.

Of course, the relational culture has its limits too. It depends very much on the quality and stability of its top talented leaders. Until the number of "organizers" of all stripes increases dramatically, it cannot replicate its successes with the kind of range and at the kind of scale necessary to make broad and lasting change. Even with many more practitioners, its rate of growth will be deliberate because of the very craftlike nature of this work. It requires constant attention—disorganizing and reorganizing—or it will slide into a bureaucratic pattern or be taken over by opportunistic market forces or simply cease to exist. And it has to fight constantly the temptations toward isolation, self-righteousness, and cults of charismatic personality.

CHAPTER II

Fault Lines and Collisions

We are trained to think in polarities—in points and counterpoints. Democrat versus Republican. Left versus right. Black versus white. But the major stresses in our society don't come in neat pairs. They reflect the collisions of at least three powerful plates. These points and moments of contact create new dangers and new opportunities for those concerned about the shape and direction of our country.

New American Cities and Suburbs

The older American cities of the northeast and Midwest must be rethought and rebuilt. They will never be as dense, as industrial or as dominant as they once were. In case anyone has any lingering doubts, just ride up I-95 and watch the moving vans lumbering out of Philadelphia, Baltimore, Bridgeport, or Trenton on a sunny fall day. The market's focus has been outward—toward the open land and relaxed zoning of the distant suburbs. The bureaucracy's focus has been inward—on holding onto the schools, hospitals, and other public institutions that remain bases of patronage in cities while the neighborhoods continue to thin. The bureaucratic culture within communities has led to the creation of scores of small, local, community development corporations that vie with one another for governmental grants and sometimes create clusters of new construction in cities that continue to sag. The so-called "public-private" solution—which has come to mean public subsidy for private gain—has been to build hotels, sports complexes, and inner harbors that appeal to tourists but do nothing for the working residents and struggling homeowners of the surrounding cities.

Our answer—an answer arrived at after decades of painful trial and error—includes a mix of market, governmental, and relational remedies. We believe that cities must organize and fund the massive removal of blight to unlock the one hidden asset they retain: land. They must demolish scores of thousands of abandoned properties. They must acquire and clear title to hundreds of acres of land. They must clean contaminated sites and relocate families from structures that are dilapidated and beyond repair. They must see themselves as aggressively competing with the suburbs and distant counties for the attention of commercial and residential, for-profit and nonprofit, builders. This work will require the kind of intensity, relentlessness, and commitment to quality that the NYPD adopted when it applied its Compstat strategy to the reduction of crime.

But once the sites have been prepared, cities must act in a very nonbureaucratic way. They must set aside significant sites and allow the market to make some of its own choices about what to build and where to build. Private sector builders have always claimed that the only things keeping them from redeveloping urban areas were the lack of land and the interference and incompetence of government agencies. It will be time for the market to put up or shut up.

Our organizations have vital roles to play. They must force a conceptual breakthrough—a new third option that differs from the two tired options of more suburban sprawl and more urban shrinkage. They must agitate for political breakthroughs in city halls and city councils filled with officials who have learned that they can continue to survive and thrive, even as their cities and their school systems decline and die. Once the blight removal work is underway, they must keep the state and market accountable. And, finally, selectively, they must show the other sectors how to build affordably, at scale, for the next generation of bus drivers and nurses, cops and teachers, who will fill the new homes and revitalize the new streets of future American cities. Older American cities will attract townhouse developments and low-rise office parks and will begin to look more like suburbs. Suburbs will stop sprawling, settle down, and feel more like cities.

New American Schools

The bureaucratic culture, dug in deeply in one of its most change resistant bunkers, has failed to create satisfactory public schools—both in cities and, increasingly, in suburbs. Private companies will expand their share of the education "market" in the coming years. Their menacing presence in the field of education and the pressure they apply on boards of education amount to an unintended public service. But the market culture lacks the interest and the patience to pick up a major portion of this social slack. There are simply too many easier and quicker ways to make money than running sixty of Philadelphia's failing public schools.

Citizens' organizations with a relational approach are just beginning to feel their way into this astonishing vacuum. In the southwest, IAF organizations and leaders are successfully applying the universals of effective organizing—individual meetings, the training and development of leaders, a process of house meetings and action and evaluation, a savvy analysis of the tendencies of the bureaucracy and the market—to the creation of teams of talented parents and school staff focused on improving the performance of struggling schools. In the northeast, our organizations are playing larger roles in the growing movement to create either new charter schools or smaller, refounded public schools. This disorganizing and reorganizing of educational patterns may give organized people an opportunity to reverse a generation-long decline in school quality and student achievement.

New American Work

The nature and value of modern work—what workers should do, what they should be paid, how they should be trained—are open to debate. Peter Drucker wrote an essay in *The Public Interest* several years ago about the growing division of labor into two large categories—service workers and knowledge workers. I wrote him and argued that there was a third category: relational workers. He responded, "You are absolutely right—but they (relational workers) consider themselves knowledge workers." Of course, they do, in the current environment, where only two choices are available. But the best of these workers, perhaps a majority of them, did not enter their professions to be supervisors or administrators, or simply to put in their years until vested for their pensions. They wanted to teach and to heal, protect and coach. They imagined themselves *relating* to people, helping people, even saving people. They started with an instinct to work directly to the individuals and families who would be their customers.

A renewed sense of relational work as an honored profession, as it is now regarded in the police, fire, and emergency service agencies of New York and Washington after September 11, as it could again be applied to teaching and nursing, social work and child care, would vastly improve the lives of those doing the work and those affected by these workers. An unlimited market exists for the training and developing of these professionals—both here and abroad, both Americans and committed relational workers from other countries.

This new American export (which sure beats the favored American export of the eighties: conflict resolution) has hardly been explored. Large portions of the world lack the most basic elements of a decent society and adequate economy. A decade of unprecedented prosperity in the west has done about as much good in the third world as Camden Yards baseball field has done in the ghettoes of East Baltimore. Skilled relational workers must plow the social ground in scores of third world countries desperate for security, schooling, health care, and social services that prepare people for self-sufficiency. Solutions that start in the third sector and public sector will set the stage for democracy's entrance and the market's entrance in vast tracts of the globe. But this all-important predevelopment, premarket, prepolitical work has hardly been imagined, much less organized, much less funded, much less done. And this task, a global New Deal that would dwarf the last one, will require the best talents and skills of more than a few thousand new field agents and security analysts at Langley.

New American Wages

Clearly, the question of what less skilled work is worth is still up for grabs. The current minimum wage keeps workers marginal and dependent on government for an alphabet soup of programs and subsidies just to survive. The expanding governmental habit of contracting out services to companies that pay low or minimum wages saves nothing in the long run. Organized labor, still in a free fall, cannot lead the charge to reverse this trend. Organized citizens, with new associations of low-wage workers, can, and already have. Here lies one of the great American fault lines, where the plates collide, where the market pushes hard, where the state retreats and offers more programs, and where organized citizens resist and insist on a living family wage.

A New Sense of Time and Scale

After a breakthrough meeting with the mayor of a major city recently, a leader remarked that it had taken so long—*ten years!*—to maneuver the organization into the center of power. I thought for a moment and then begged to differ. In ten years, we had gone from nothing—no money, no member institutions, no leaders, no training, and no recognition—to a remarkable meeting with a formerly recalcitrant mayor over the most important decision that the city would be making during his administration. This pace, in fact, was *fast*, particularly if the meeting and discussion resulted in a unique approach to removing blight and rebuilding an urban wasteland. The arc of recovery and revitalization is long—longer than the eight years a president may serve, longer than the increasingly shorter periods before reelection campaigns, longer than the terms served by ambitious and distracted mayors, far longer than the quarterly, monthly, or weekly updates scrutinized by shareholders in the market. In fact, neither the market nor the bureaucratic cultures are suited to the challenges and the demands of social and human development. Only the steady and restless leaders of mature citizens power organizations—and other third sector groups—are ideally positioned for it.

Those leaders, and many more like them, as remarkable as they already are, need to think bigger and be bolder than they have been in the past. Those who work for a living, who are struggling to raise kids, who are stuck in traffic on the turnpike every day, who are watching people losing their jobs in neighboring cubicles, who have sons and daughters in the military overseas, who are approaching retirement after thirty or thirty-five years of hard and steady labor, still would like to believe that the people they elect and the administrators they pay who serve in the public sector will address the glaring gaps in our country and beyond. Or they secretly wish the hype they hear incessantly chanted by the mullahs of the market were true—or at least truer. At the end of the day, they wouldn't mind it at all if the world were more as it should be, not as it is.

In the world as it is, the *scale* of change, like the pace, is beyond the reach of most modern bureaucracies and not yet attractive to the market. Building thirty homes may satisfy those in the foundation or housing establishments but does nothing for the long term recovery of a community. Building three thousand homes may antagonize the housing and funding establishments but totally reclaims an abandoned community. Working with teams of leaders in five schools may be worthy. But only the presence of one hundred teams in one hundred schools will generate the critical mass of participation and accountability needed to transform a failing school system. The challenge to the new leaders of the relational third sector is to have the courage and persistence to hit issues hard enough, high enough, and long enough to make a significant and enduring difference.

Pick your interest or public passion. Evaluate the ways the market culture and bureaucratic culture have performed. And then just try to convince me that there is not a role for crafty and capable leaders, well organized and comfortable with power, rooted in a third sector that is working at its relational best.

CHAPTER 12

The Right Relationship

The market remains dominant—although the attacks of 11 September reminded all Americans of its limits. The market could not and would not subvert its own interests to protect the nation by readily surrendering its contracts to provide airport security on the cheap. A government capable of putting public safety above profit had to intervene. And citizens in relationship to one another, in burning buildings and hijacked planes, in devastated communities and mourning congregations, rose to the challenges of those terrible hours and days. Not motivated by profit or distracted by pecking order, they led, just as hard-pressed bands of soldiers led in the first chaotic hours on Omaha Beach, just as moderate African-American citizens led by sitting in forbidden seats on buses in Birmingham.

We still haven't worked out the best mix of each culture in our own institutions and in society as a whole. How *should* it look? Government agencies that enhance the health, education, and security of citizens should be lauded. Those that don't should be disorganized and reorganized. This will only occur when top political and agency leaders work closely with organized citizens on a consistent basis. The market must either learn to restrain itself at times or adjust itself to more powerful and more persuasive pressure from organized citizens. The market has done a better job than any other economic system at enabling people to take advantage of opportunity, to build equity, and to improve and prosper. It undercuts itself and exposes itself to constraint and regulation when it shirks its institutional responsibility to its employees and communities, when it contradicts its own rhetoric by angling for governmental subsidies, and when it strips working families of their hard-earned wealth whenever times get tight. The relational leaders of the third sector cannot just wait for the next catastrophe to show their stuff. They must marshal their forces, train well, and take the fight to those who seem content to live in a nation that still has millions, and a world that has billions, of decent but desperate have-nots, yearning to work hard and raise their families, eager to live in peace and breathe free.

CONCLUSION

As you may have guessed by now, I enjoy this life of action and tension, conflict and forward motion.

I enjoy it for its own sake—for the dryness in the mouth and the butterflies in the belly in the moments before a particularly pivotal meeting with a mayor.

I enjoy it because organizing provides me with an unlimited political MetroCard: it permits travel into every corner of every city, into every class, and into every racial and ethnic precinct in our extraordinarily diverse world.

I enjoy it because I find myself standing, on a chilly morning, in a circle of leaders, outside City Hall, in the lobby of a major bank, on a hillside in South Africa, among people I appreciate and admire and respect, people who often challenge me and who respond to my challenge of them, people who are such innovative social and political entrepreneurs.

I enjoy it when I walk down streets filled with homes that our groups have built, when I enter schools or after-school programs that exist because of the power and pressure of BUILD in Baltimore or South Bronx Churches, when I trace the rising reading and math scores of schools in Texas where our organized parents participate fully and play productive roles, when I drive past a pool and park packed with kids that was rebuilt because of the guts and guile of Alice McCollum, when I see more cops and fewer thugs, more winning and less whining.

I enjoy it because organizing offers me a way to exercise the freedoms my father fought so hard to preserve and my mother, alone now in her small home on the northwest side of Chicago, still reading and thinking and alive to events in the changed and changing world around her, still does her part to sustain.

My understanding of power and politics, about the responsibilities and opportunities of American citizenship, started with them, in the home we owned on Ferdinand Street, in the stories they told about immigration, the Great Depression, and the war, in the way they lived their lives. Even in death, my father kept teaching lessons in dignity and loyalty. His gravestone, in St. Adalbert Cemetery, on the northwest side of Chicago, reads: "August Gecan, Sergeant, U.S. Army."

And my thinking was shaped by the fire that killed the children of Our Lady of the Angels school, along with the smoldering fires that burned across scores of American cities and hundreds of American neighborhoods for nearly two decades. Fire prevention and fire safety mean more to me than protecting individual buildings from catastrophe. They mean protecting ourselves and our loved ones from the carelessness of our own institutions, from the sometimes blind and destructive attacks of the market, from the blundering and belated responses of bureaucracies, from the reality of evil and the vulnerability of those who cannot yet counter power with power.

The birth of my own children carried some of the smoke from the fire at OLA away.

The rebuilding of East Brooklyn and other communities assuaged the grief that grew from witnessing the destruction of so many magnificent American communities.

The intelligence and intensity and wonder in the faces of leaders engaged in action channeled the anger provoked by the worship of wealth and celebrity and the clutter of DO NOT ENTER signs.

As I finish this book, the rubble still smolders in lower Manhattan. Soon that fire will be out. But the pall of smoke, so large it could be seen by American astronauts circling the earth, will linger decades longer.

We must deter, capture, or fight to the death the terrorists who came out of the sky to murder innocent Americans on a September morning and the terrorists who lurk in the shadows of unlighted stairwells on forgotten streets. But *as* we do that and *after* we do that, we must rebuild the schools and towers, cities and countries, physically and socially and politically, that enemies from without or enemies from within have conspired to destroy.

This is the work of a generation. It beckons all those many millions of Americans who wonder when they will be called, where they will be tested, and how they can create their own lasting legacy in the country and the world that we wrestle with and love.

ACKNOWLEDGMENTS

In 1963, quite by accident, at the casual suggestion of grade school friend Ron Rolewicz, I tagged along with him and took the entrance exam to St. Ignatius High School. I passed the test and ended up "leaving the neighborhood," as we used to say. I traveled by bus and el, about eight miles, to one of the great educational institutions in the nation. I had more good luck when I sat in the same row as Dan Flanagan, Jim Hinsdale, and Terry Flynn, and across the room from Rick Roche. They came from exotic places— Oak Park, Westchester, Hyde Park, and the mysterious kingdom called the South Side—with wide and rich views of the world. We explored those and other worlds together, with Terry usually leading the way.

Through the years, I have had the privilege to meet and work with religious men and women of extraordinary talent and courage. The unofficial dean of this group is the Reverend Vernon Dobson, of Union Baptist Church, in Baltimore. Reverend Dobson is the largely anonymous heir of the mantle of leadership that started with the Reverend Vernon Johns, and passed to Dr. Martin

Luther King Jr. Reverend Dobson still does it all, ministering, serving, organizing, and occasionally, almost literally, breathing fire when he speaks. Anyone within range of his resonant voice, friend or foe, tends to stop and listen. He and Arnie Graf, my friend, colleague, and coconspirator, have anchored our work in the northeast region for the past twenty-five years. When the winds roared and waves rose, they remained steady and strong.

Reverend Dobson has surrounded himself with a talented group of younger leaders, black and white, in still-bleeding Baltimore. Reverend Doug Miles and Curtis Jones, Fr. Joe Muth and Roger Guench, are just four of many. Msgr. Claire O'Dwyer, a tall, lean, larger-than-life veteran of the Civil Rights years, has been dead for many years but has never been far from our thoughts.

Thirty miles south, in Washington, another team of leaders is at work. Washington is a terrible town to get political traction in. The gum and glue ooze from Capitol Hill into every municipal pore. But pastors like Lionel Edmonds and Luis Leon, Darryl Macklin and Joe Daniels, and lay leaders like Carol Wheeler and John More have gotten the District moving again. They have known when to push and pressure, as well as when to lighten up and laugh. I'll always treasure the laughter.

I have had the privilege work with some of the country's finest priest and sisters—John Peyton and Jim Spengler, Frances Gritte and Regina Fuhrmann, Bruce Lewandowski and John Grange, Alice Reichmeider and Peter Gavigan, Neil Connelly and Mary Ann McHugh, David Garcia and Jim Cavanaugh, John Mc-Namee and Cecile Reilly, Eileen Trainer and Charlie Plock. They have given all and risked everything, in the toughest of places, in the leanest of times, without much fuss—and still do, on a daily basis, without much support.

If you are in any city where we organize, you can find these estimable leaders. They come in all denominations and most faiths. In

Philadelphia, there is Fr. Isaac Miller, Reverend Peter Sime, Rabbi Avi Winokur, and Reverend Reed Brinkman, among others. In Boston, there is Msgr. Frank Kelly and Fr. John Doyle. In Queens, there is Reverend Patrick O'Connor and Fr. John Amann. In Brooklyn, you'll meet Reverend David Brawley, Reverend Ernest L. White, and Reverend Nils Blatz. In Long Island, Pastor Tom Pranschke and Sr. Evelyn Lamoureux work. In Manhattan, Fr. Earl Koopercamp and Reverend Jim Speer. This list, quite literally, could go for many more pages.

In the noisy and treacherous intersection where housing and finance and politics collide, several savvy and talented people have served as traffic cops and guides: Mike Lappin, Felice Michetti, and Hugh Kelly in New York, along with Jeremy Nowak and the late Corliss Young in Philadelphia knew which risks to take and which collisions to avoid. Like the Old Testament figure Nehemiah, they knew that you needed to build with a trowel in one hand and a sword in the other. In the gray and Byzantine world of public education, I have watched bright and unstoppable organizers like Ray Domanico and Kim Zalent, Lee Stuart and Katherine Kelly, light the way.

I have written a book from my perspective, with stories that occurred in New York, Philadelphia, Baltimore, and Chicago. Even when I have described situations in those places, I have left out people who played pivotal roles. Msgr. John Egan and Jack Macnamara helped build and run the Contract Buyers League in Chicago. But they never would have succeeded without the grit and smarts of Peter Welch and Mark Splain, Jim Devanney and Dave Quammen, Maureen McDonald and Ward Ghory, Alan Boles and Joe Putnick, Joe Speier and Bill Ford, and the legal skills of Tom Sullivan, Tom Boodell, and Gerry and Patty Randolph. Decades after this group finished its important work and closed up shop, the leaders and staff held a commemorative meeting. More

[182] Acknowledgments

than three hundred people attended, an urban VFW gathering of veterans happy to remember a war that ended in a partial victory.

All books need focus. And I focused on the work of the IAF in the northeast primarily. Other organizers have other books within them. I've listened to their stories and marveled at their work for more than two decades. I hope that Sr. Christine Stephens and Elizabeth Valdez, Sr. Pearl Cesar and Frank Pierson each write theirs about their work in Texas and Arizona. The same goes for Dick Harmon in Oregon and Gerald Taylor in North Carolina, Maribeth Larkin in Los Angeles and Lottie Sneed in Washington, Louise Green in New York and Stephen Roberson in Chicago, Tom Holler in Nebraska and Ken Smith in California. Ernesto Cortes and Ed Chambers have a couple of books each within them.

Younger and more recent organizers are beginning to write their own chapters. Watch for these names: Rob English, Coleman Milling, and Mark Fraley in Maryland; Van Jones and Judy Donovan in Texas; Marielys Divanne in the Bronx; and Cheri Andes in Boston. Or, better yet, if you are interested in this work, join them.

Even crusty organizers occasionally need support and encouragement. I've received more than my share. In the foundation world, not my favorite place to be, Maddy Lee has been a fine teacher. Georgianna Gleason, Sharon King, John Moyer, Sue Chinn, Marcia Smith, Fred Davie, Pam Stebbins, and Fr. Jamie Calloway have all been fair, balanced, and full of good humor. I would rather hear no from them than yes from some others. (A yes from them is better yet.) Lucille Clark, the elegant and resourceful administrative director of East Brooklyn Congregations, has been a great partner and associate for more than twenty years. She typed all of the early concept papers that described our dream of rebuilding the East Brooklyn neighborhood she called home—and believed that it would come to pass. Margaret McKenzie, who plays the same role for the IAF, has mastered the art of running creative actions on organizers who get a little too full of themselves. She agitates the agitators on a regular basis.

The IAF's board of directors has allowed us to do our occasionally risky and often controversial work without a hint of the anxiety that we know they have felt. Marv Wurth has been a fine and steady president. Dr. Jean Bethke Elshtain and AME Bishop John Hurst Adams, Talat Othman, Episcopal Bishop Hays Rockwell, and Barry Menuez have not so much kept us in line as they have enabled us to do our work on the front lines. Jean Elshtain was kind enough to invite me to give a talk five summers ago at the Chautauqua Institution. Many of the original themes included in this book were given a trial spin on a steamy morning in upstate New York.

Along the way, remarkable organizers moved into other fields or continued their organizing work with other institutions. Larry McNeil and Dave Nelson, Steve Pulkkinen and Zeik Saidman, Dave Fleischer and Jessica Govea, Bob Moriarity and Josh Hoyt and Kathleen O'Toole all made important contributions, and still do. Tom Mosgaller of Madison, Wisconsin, and I still keep up an old tradition of talking late on Sunday nights. Two great friends and exceptional citizens, Elyse Pivnick and Norm Glickman, keep trying to convince me of the untapped potential of technology. I've been a dull student and grudging convert, but I have always appreciated their energy and resolve. Another good friend, Fran Barrett, encouraged me to take a second look at some people. I always listened to Fran, the soul of New York.

I published my last book, essays written by fellow college students that I edited, thirty years ago. What I had heard over the years about the world of publishing was that it had become much more corporate, cutthroat, and commercial. My experience may be the exception that proves the rule. Authors and journalists—Sam Freedman, Bill Greider, Wayne Barrett, Tom Robbins, Bob Laird, and the indefatigable Janice Fine—could not have been more generous with their time and support. At times, I felt a little guilty, not able to match their enthusiasm, particularly Sam's and Janice's, with enough consistency of effort. The people at the Beacon Press, executive editor Deb Chasman, publisher Helene Atwan, and editorial assistant Julie Hassel have been terrific. Every writer should have the good fortune to work with an editor like Deb Chasman, who made suggestion after suggestion, gently but firmly, that improved this book. And every writer should have friends like Goldie and Mary Sherrill, Mary Wilke and Steve Curtin, who provided a warm welcome during several cold New Hampshire nights.

These pages are the product of a family, as much as a single person. My mother, Mary Gecan, used to leave "good" books, like Dickens's *A Tale of Two Cities,* scattered around our Ferdinand Street house in Chicago, when my sister and I were not yet in our teens. At some point, I picked them up and started to read. I've never stopped. My uncle Nick and aunt Babe, who formed the hub of our community, always told wonderful and magical stories. They lived hard lives and still managed to love the world—an art and a gift. Their daughter, Cathy, and my sister Barbara, along with Barb's husband, Kazem Nemazee, have provided the consistent presence and loving care that my mother, aunt, and uncle all deserve. I wish my father were here and could read this. When people used to ask him what I did for a living, he would never say that I was an organizer. Instead, he'd proudly announce, "Michael builds houses!" Now he might have added, "And he writes books!"

My own children—Joseph, Alex, and Nora—are all wonderful, supple writers. They would come home from school and find me staring at the computer screen. They would often ask whether or not I had gone to work that day. "No," I'd say, "I've been working, here, trying to write this book." Each of them, separately, without consulting, said, "Come on, dad, writing isn't work!" In a particularly challenging period, Nora, just twelve, wrote a poem, titled "Hope," and left it on the kitchen counter for me when I woke up early the next morning. I carry it and a piece written by Alex and Joe wherever I go.

Finally, every word of every draft was read by my wife, Sheila Morrissey. She made scores, maybe hundreds, of helpful comments in the margins. When I got a little carried away, she just drew a light line through much of the wonderful, irreplaceable prose that is no longer a part of this book. When I thought I was done with a section, I'd leave it on the dining room table and pretend not to be completely preoccupied with her review and judgment. Thumbs-down was delivered this way, "It needs a little more work." Thumbs-up was even shorter, "That's it." In the midst of a difficult period, with health and other traumas hitting every couple of months or so, Sheila remained thoroughly positive, never flagged, and carried me along. This is as much her work as mine, as is everything else in my life since we met thirty-three years ago.

INDEX

REVEILLE FOR RADICALS

by Saul Alinsky

First published in 1946 and updated in 1969 with a new introduction and afterword, this volume represents the fullest
statement of the political philosophy and practical methodolo-
gy of one of the most important figures in the history of
American radicalism. Like Thomas Paine before him, Saul
Alinsky, through the concept and practice of community organizing, was able to embody for his era both the urgency of
radical political action and the imperative of rational political
discourse. His work and writing bequeathed a new method
and style of social change to American communities that will
remain a permanent part of the American political landscape.

Political Science/0-679-72112-6

RULES FOR RADICALS

A Pragmatic Primer for Realistic Radicals

by Saul Alinsky

First published in 1971, *Rules for Radicals* is Saul Alinsky's
impassioned call for young radicals on how to effect constructive social change and know "the difference between being a
realistic radical and being a rhetorical one." Written in the midst
of political developments whose direction Alinsky was the first
to question, this volume exhibits his style at its best. Saul
Alinsky was able to combine, both in his person and in his
writing, the intensity of political engagement with an absolute
insistence on rational political discourse and adherence to the
American democratic tradition.

Political Science/0-679-72113-4